RIGHTS TO LIGHT

Sarah Hannaford QC,

Jessica Stephens

and

Rachael O'Hagan

Acknowledgments

Crown copyright material is reproduced with the permission of the Controller of HMSO and the Queen's Printer for Scotland.

Please note: References to the masculine include, where appropriate, the feminine.

Published by the Royal Institution of Chartered Surveyors (RICS)
Surveyor Court
Westwood Business Park
Coventry CV4 8JE
UK
www.ricsbooks.com

ISBN 978 1 84219 153 8

Typeset in Great Britain by Columns Design Ltd, Reading, Berks

Printed in Great Britain by Page Bros, Milecross Lane, Norwich

Contents

Preface

While chartered surveyors may not need the breadth of understanding of the law of their opposite numbers in the legal profession, in a number of key areas of application to property and construction they need a similar depth of legal knowledge. Exactly what the key areas may be depends to some extent on the nature of the surveyor's practice; two obvious examples are the law of landlord and tenant and town and country planning. There are plenty of chartered surveyors who know much more about rent reviews or compulsory purchase compensation than the average lawyer in general practice. They need to know the law as much as the valuation principles, not least because the former can affect the latter.

So surveyors require legal knowledge and for a variety of reasons need to develop their understanding of it. Changing trends or individual variations in clients' requirements mean that from time to time even the best practitioners (perhaps especially the best practitioners) will feel the need to expand their knowledge. The knowledge acquired at college or in study for the Assessment of Professional Competence has a limited shelf life and needs to be constantly updated to maintain its currency. Even specialists working in their areas of expertise need a source of reference as an aide-memoire or as a first port of call in more detailed research.

The Case in Point series

RICS Books is committed to meeting the needs of surveying (and other) professionals and the Case in Point series typifies that commitment. It is aimed at those who need to upgrade or update their legal knowledge, or who need to have access to a good first reference at the outset of an inquiry. A particular difficulty in doing so lies in the area of case law. Chartered surveyors are generally well aware of the importance of case law but are confronted by a significant practical problem in dealing with it, namely, the burgeoning of reported decisions of the courts. The sheer scale of the law reports, both general and specialist, makes it very hard even to be aware of recent trends, let alone identify the significance of a particular decision. Thus it was decided to focus on the developments in case law. In any given matter, the practitioner will want to be directed efficiently to the decision which bears upon the matter with which he or she is dealing; in other words, to the 'case in point'.

The series has developed incrementally since its launch in 2002 and now comprises 15 books covering a wide range of legal subjects affecting the work of chartered surveyors. As well as property investment/management areas such as *Rent Review* and *Lease Renewal* and pure construction subjects such as *Construction Claims and Adjudication*, there are some titles relevant to all disciplines, such as *Expert Witness* and *Party Walls*, the latter also by Sarah Hannaford and Jessica Stephens. It is indicative of the strength of demand and the success of the series that new titles are appearing and still being commissioned at the same time as the first 2nd editions, on *Negligence in Surveys and Valuations* and *Service Charges*, are published.

The author of each title has the degree of expertise required to be selective and succinct, thus achieving a high degree of relevancy without sacrificing accessibility, so that busy practitioners get what they need – the law on the matter they are handling, when they want it.

Rights to light

It is axiomatic that, in increasingly densely populated urban environments, the impact of neighbouring properties upon each other grows. The law has to regulate the rights and obligations of owners and occupiers of land and buildings and this role becomes more crucial as the 'flash-points' become more numerous and more significant. Rights to light is a classic example of an area of the law where the truth of these statements is evident. It is a natural companion volume to *Party Walls* and *Easements and Other Rights* in the Case in Point series. In one sense, this book is a development of the latter, since a right to light in the legal sense can only be enforced in the form of an easement; there is no such thing as a generally applicable right to light. However, the layman's expectation is often to that effect and the legally enforceable right itself makes the right to light a highly contentious and even emotive subject. Professional advisers, notably in property management and development, know that the existence, extent and enforceability of a right to light can of itself make the difference between profitability and non-viability of a project.

So it is not surprising that a considerable body of case law has built up over the years. This is dealt with by reference to acquisition of rights (whether by grant, reservation or prescription), extinguishment, infringement and enforcement. To the many classic authorities are added major new decisions of the courts, such as *Midtown v City of London Real Property Co*, *Tamares (Vincent Square) v Fairpoint Properties* and *Regan v Paul Properties Ltd*. The coverage includes a welcome chapter on a separate though related issue, that of high hedges, such as leylandii, now subject to recent statutory regulation under the *Anti-social Behaviour Act* 2003 and the *High Hedges (Appeals) (England) Regulations* 2005.

The authors' treatment of rights to light is essentially practical. Although some of the law is conceptually difficult and analysis of principle is unavoidable, users of this book will typically wish to know the meaning and legal status of the 50/50 rule, whether the layout of a building is significant or what remedies are available for infringement of rights.

RICS Books has been fortunate to obtain the services of authors from Keating Chambers who are able to provide practical answers to these and many other questions through the case law. Keating Chambers is a specialist set dealing with all aspects of construction, property development and management disputes.

Sarah Hannaford QC was called to the Bar in 1989 and took silk in 2008. Also well known for her expertise in construction procurement, she is a specialist in party walls and rights to light issues.

Jessica Stephens was called to the Bar in 2001 and as well as her mainstream construction work has developed a niche practice in party wall, easement and boundary disputes, including rights to light.

Sarah Hannaford and Jessica Stephens co authored the RICS *Case in Point Party Walls* title in 2004.

Rachael O'Hagan is a graduate of the University of Birmingham and has spent two years as a Legal Assistant at Keating Chambers prior to commencing pupillage.

Their combined expertise and skills have made a difficult area of case law accessible and readily applicable to practical situations.

Anthony Lavers
Professional Support Lawyer, White & Case LLP, London
Visiting Professor of Law, Oxford Brookes University
Consultant Editor, Case in Point series

List of Acts and abbreviations

The following Acts are referenced in this publication. Where an Act is mentioned frequently, it is referred to by the abbreviation that follows the name of the Act in brackets.

Anti-social Behaviour Act 2003 (**'ASBA 2003'**)
Chancery Amendment Act 1858
Civil Procedure Rules 1998 (SI 1998/3132)
Compulsory Purchase Act 1965
Conveyancing Act 1881
County Courts Act 1984
Environment Protection Act 1990
High Hedges (Appeals) (England) Regulations 2005 (SI 2005/711)
High Hedges (Appeals) (Wales) Regulations 2004 (SI 2004/3240) (W 282)
Housing Act 1985
Land Clauses Consolidation Act 1845
Land Registration Act 2002
Land Tribunal Rules 1996 (SI 1996/1022)
Law of Property Act 1925 (**'LPA 1925'**)
Law of Property (Miscellaneous Provisions) Act 1989
Party Walls etc. Act 1996
Prescription Act 1832 (**'the *Prescription Act*'**)
Railway Clauses Act 1845
Regional Development Agencies Act 1998
Rights of Light Act 1959
Supreme Court Act 1981
Town And Country Planning Act 1990

The text of this publication is divided into commentary and case summaries. The commentary is enclosed between grey highlighted lines for ease of reference.

Table of Cases

1
Introduction

1.1 WHAT IS A RIGHT TO LIGHT?

A right to light is a building owner's or occupier's right to receive light through windows or other apertures in his property across adjacent land.

The right relates to light received by a building and not by vacant land or by a garden.

Potts v Smith (1868)

The plaintiff claimed that the defendant's new building interfered with the free access of light and air to his garden. The judge stated that:

> '... in the present case, and in all others, it must be well understood that, however agreeable and beautiful a garden may be, if another person has land immediately adjoining it, neither the pleasure derived from the scent or sight of the flowers will prevent the owner of the adjoining land from erecting whatever buildings on his land he thinks fit.'

A right to light does not protect the right to a particular view. An owner or occupier of property cannot therefore complain if an obstruction is created on adjoining land which affects the view from his windows.

Bland v Moseley Trinity (1587)

The judge stated:

> 'But ... for prospect, which is a matter only of delight and not of necessity, no action lies for stopping thereof, and yet it is a great commendation of a house if it has a long and large prospect ... But the law does not give an action for such things of delight.'

Phipps v Pears (1965)

Summarising the law, Lord Denning MR said:

> 'Suppose you have a fine view from your house. You have enjoyed the view for many years. It adds greatly to the value of your house. But if your neighbour chooses to despoil it, by building up and blocking it, you have no redress. There is no such right known to the law as a right to a prospect or view ... The only way in which you can keep the view from your house is to get your neighbour to make a covenant with you that he will not build so as to block your view.'

1.2 THE LEGAL NATURE OF A RIGHT TO LIGHT

A right to light falls into a category of legal rights known as easements. Easements are rights over or in relation to the land of another person. Other easements include rights of way and rights of support. Easements can be either 'positive' or 'negative': a right to light is a negative easement.

Easements have four important characteristics.

Re Ellenborough Park; Powell v Maddison (1956)

The Court of Appeal set out the four characteristics essential to an easement:

(1) There must be a dominant and a servient tenement.

(2) An easement must accommodate the dominant tenement.

(3) Dominant and servient owners must be different persons.

(4) A right over land cannot amount to an easement unless it is capable of forming the subject matter of a grant.

These characteristics apply to rights to light:

- In rights to light cases, there must be a dominant and a servient tenement (or property). In this book, the phrases 'dominant property' and 'servient property' are used. The land over which the right is exercised is known as the servient property. The land which has the benefit of the right is known as the dominant property. Dominant and servient properties adjoin or are in close proximity to one another.

- The right to light must benefit the dominant property and not simply the person owning it.
- For an easement to exist, the two properties must be in separate ownership. However, in the case of rights to light, it is not always necessary for there to be different freehold owners, if one property is, or both properties are, leased (see 3.4.7 below).
- It has been recognised, at least since the House of Lords' decision in *Dalton v Angus* (1881), that a right to light fulfils the fourth characteristic of an easement. It is capable of forming the subject matter of a grant (i.e. is a right which the law recognises one owner may grant to another).

1.3 HOW IS A RIGHT TO LIGHT ACQUIRED?

There are a number of ways in which a right to light can be acquired:

- It can be deliberately created by express words in a conveyance, a lease or an agreement by deed.
- Without the use of express words, a right to light can sometimes be implied into a conveyance or lease.
- A right to light can be acquired by prescription, i.e. by use (sometimes called 'user') over a number of years. There are three different methods of prescription:
  - at common law,
  - under the doctrine of lost modern grant, and
  - under the *Prescription Act* 1832.

The different methods by which a right to light can be acquired are discussed in detail in Chapters 2 and 3.

1.4 CAN A RIGHT TO LIGHT BE LOST?

There are various ways in which a right to light may be lost. These include extinguishment by agreement, by the ownership of the dominant and servient properties being united, by abandonment, by statute and if substantial alterations are made to the dominant property. The different ways in which rights can be lost are discussed in Chapter 4.

1.5 WHAT REMEDIES ARE AVAILABLE FOR INFRINGEMENT OF RIGHTS TO LIGHT?

A right to light is not the right to *all* the light which a property receives. It is a right to sufficient light for the comfortable use and enjoyment of the house or place of business. Surveyors conventionally measure whether the light left to the dominant property is sufficient by using the 50/50 rule (which is discussed in Chapter 5). If an adjacent development reduces the level of light below this standard, the dominant owner's primary remedies will be either an injunction (to prevent the infringement or, if the building has been constructed, to require it to be pulled down) or damages. Injunctions can be awarded either before the trial (so as to prevent the building proceeding pending the court's decision at trial) or at the end of the trial. They are not always easy to obtain. The issues arising in relation to claims for injunctions and damages are discussed in Chapter 7.

1.6 THE NEED FOR REFORM

Much of the law relating to rights to light is very old. Parties still frequently rely on cases decided in the 19th century or early in the 20th century. The law on prescription is particularly old. The doctrine of lost modern grant, despite its name, came into being in the 17th and 18th centuries and the *Prescription Act* dates back to 1832. In addition, the law (particularly on the acquisition and extinguishment of rights to light) is complicated and can be confusing. For example, the existence of three different methods of acquiring a right to light by prescription, each with different criteria, is confusing and unnecessary.

There is little doubt that the law relating to rights to light (and easements generally) needs reform. Both the courts and commentators have frequently criticised it. For example, in relation to prescription the Law Reform Committee in 1966 stated that the:

> 'Prescription Act 1832 has no friends. It has been long criticised as one of the worst drafted Acts on the Statute Book.'

The Court of Appeal in *Tehidy Minerals Ltd v Norman* (1971) expressed a similar concern, saying:

> 'The co-existence of three separate methods of prescribing is, in our view, anomalous and undesirable, for it results in much unnecessary complication and confusion. We hope that it may be possible for the Legislature to effect a long-overdue simplification in this branch of the law.'

More recently, in March 2008, the Law Commission reviewed the law of easements in its Consultation Paper no. 186. The Paper is critical of the law of easements generally and identifies possible changes on which the Law Commission has launched a consultation. Suggested areas of reform which are particularly relevant to rights to light disputes include the law on:

- the implied acquisition of easements;
- the acquisition of easements by prescription; and
- extinguishment of easements.

Developments in the law of rights to light are therefore currently awaited.

2
Acquisition

2.1 INTRODUCTION

A right to light can be acquired by:

- express grant or reservation;
- implied grant or reservation; or
- prescription.

This chapter deals with acquisition by grant or reservation. Acquisition by prescription is covered in Chapter 3.

2.2 ACQUISITION BY EXPRESS GRANT OR RESERVATION

2.2.1 Introduction

A right to light can be created by express words. This is usually done in a conveyance or lease. It can also be done in a document created expressly for that purpose, often called a deed of grant. Express words can be used either to grant or to reserve a right to light.

Grant: The typical situation of an express grant of a right to light arises where the owner of land sells plot A and retains plot B. He may, in the conveyance of plot A, include an express right to light for the benefit of plot A over plot B.

Reservation: The typical situation of an express reservation of a right to light also arises where the owner of land sells plot A and retains plot B. He may, in the conveyance of plot A, include an express reservation of a right to light for the benefit of plot B over plot A (so that the new owner of plot A does not build a property blocking the existing light to the property on plot B).

The following is an example of typical wording for either a grant or reservation of a right to light:

'The right to the free and unobstructed passage of light to the Premises at all times.'

2.2.2 Interpretation of an express grant or reservation

The meaning of an express grant or reservation of a right to light will depend on the words used, other terms of the document containing the grant or reservation (such as a lease or conveyance), the surrounding circumstances and commercial common sense. Unless the surrounding circumstances or other terms of the lease or conveyance lead to a different conclusion, an express grant or reservation of a right to light will entitle the owner to the degree of light which is necessary for the comfortable use and enjoyment of the property according to people's ordinary requirements. This is the same as the degree of light to which a right is acquired by prescription, as explained in *Colls v Home and Colonial Stores Ltd* (1904) (see Chapter 5).

Frogmore Developments Ltd v Shirayama Shokusan Co (1997)

The London Residuary Board (LRB) owned a site which included property known as the Riverside Building and the East Land. In October 1993, LRB leased the Riverside Building to the defendant. Clause 6 of Schedule 2 to the 1993 lease granted the defendant 'the right to the free and unobstructed passage of light and air to the Premises at all times'. LRB later transferred the freehold of a block of property, including the East Land, to the plaintiff. The transfer contained an express reservation of a right to the free and unobstructed passage of light and air to the land retained by LRB, which included the Riverside Building.

Prior to the transfer to the plaintiff, the East Land had planning permission for a development known as the Belvedere Centre. In fact, the plaintiff decided to carry out a different development. This development would not have affected light to as much of the Riverside Building as the Belvedere Centre would have done, but it would have had a more serious effect on part of the Riverside Building.

The issue of the extent of the defendant's right to light arose for decision by the court. The defendant argued that, because the Riverside Building had been granted a right to an unqualified right to light, it was entitled to the amount of light which, according to the ordinary notions of mankind, would be required for the ordinary purposes for which the Riverside Building was used, i.e. the amount of light applicable where a right to light has been acquired by prescription in accordance with *Colls v Home and Colonial Stores Ltd* (1904) (see Chapter 5). The plaintiff, however, argued that the defendant was only entitled to as much light as would have been left if the Belvedere Centre had been built, because the parties had anticipated that the Belvedere Centre, or something similar to it, would be built on the East Land. The parties agreed that the proper construction of Clause 6 of Schedule 2 of the 1993 lease turned on the wording of that Clause, the other provisions of the lease, the provisions of the agreement for lease (which had led to the lease), the surrounding circumstances and commercial common sense.

The judge found in favour of the defendant. He considered that the meaning of Clause 6 was clear. He held that it was quite obvious that the construction of the Belvedere Centre or the new building would obstruct the access of light so as to amount to a breach of the Clause. He also relied on the fact that the grant of a right to light, especially in terms as strong as Clause 6, had a well-established meaning as a term of art, namely to entitle the grantee to a degree of light which satisfied the test in *Colls v Home and Colonial Stores Ltd* (1904). Some provisions in the lease and the agreement for lease indicated that the Belvedere Centre or a similar development might be constructed on the East Land. However, he held that these provisions, the surrounding circumstances and commercial common sense did not displace the clear meaning of Clause 6.

2.2.3 Express grant by freeholder to leaseholder

A freehold owner of property A, who has acquired a right to light by prescription over neighbouring property B, can expressly grant a right to light over property B to the lessee of property A.

Midtown Ltd v City of London Real Property Company Ltd (2005)

Separate actions were brought by the freehold owner (Midtown) and leasehold owner (Kendall Freeman) of a property to the west of a site in which the defendant had a long leasehold interest and which it proposed to develop. The claimants sought injunctions, claiming that the defendant's proposed development would interfere with their rights to light. They claimed that they were both entitled to a right to light acquired by prescription under section 3 of the *Prescription Act*. The defendant admitted that Midtown was entitled to such a right but argued that Kendall Freeman could not show 20 years' enjoyment of light before the commencement of the action. Therefore, on the second day of the trial, Midtown entered into an agreement with Kendall Freeman to grant it a right to light by deed. Kendall Freeman applied to amend its claim so that it could argue that it had acquired a right to light by express grant. The judge allowed Kendall Freeman to amend.

2.2.4 Formal requirements

Rights to lights created by express words are regulated by the *Law of Property Act* 1925 (LPA 1925). This states that:

- a legal easement must be granted by deed (LPA 1925, section 52); and
- an equitable easement may be granted by a document, other than a deed, provided that it is in writing and signed (LPA 1925, section 53).

Express rights to light relating to registered land need to be registered at the Land Registry in accordance with the *Land Registration Act* 2002. The registration is made in relation to both the servient and the dominant land.

2.3 ACQUISITION BY IMPLIED GRANT

A right to light can also be created by implied grant. There are a number of ways in which an implied grant of a right to light can arise. The categories overlap and different authors have categorised them in slightly different ways. The categories can be summarised as follows:

- non-derogation from grant;
- the rule in *Wheeldon v Burrows* (1879); and
- section 62 of LPA 1925.

The principles applicable to the acquisition of a right to light by implied reservation are different from those applicable to implied grant and are dealt with separately at 2.4 below.

2.3.1 Non-derogation from grant

For well over a century, there has been an established principle that a grantor may not derogate from his grant. This means that when a person (the grantor) transfers land to another, whether by sale of the freehold or lease, he cannot do it on terms that effectively undermine the purpose of the transfer. As one Court of Appeal judge put it (in *Birmingham, Dudley and District Banking Co v Ross* (1888)), the principle is that 'a grantor having given a thing with one hand is not to take away the means of enjoying it with the other'. The courts have sometimes used this doctrine to assist in implying a right to light into a conveyance or lease.

Frederick Betts Ltd v Pickfords Ltd (1906)

The defendant occupied two adjoining plots, one of which he then leased to the plaintiff. By a covenant in the lease, the plaintiff agreed to build a warehouse on the leased plot in accordance with approved plans. The plans provided for the back wall of the warehouse to contain windows. To enable the plaintiff to build in accordance with the plans, the defendant agreed to clear the buildings which stood on the leased land and to demolish one end of a building which stood partly on the plaintiff's and partly on the defendant's land. The defendant failed satisfactorily to remove one of the buildings and as a result the local authority considered the back wall of the warehouse to be a party wall and ordered the plaintiff to block up the windows (as a party wall could not have windows).

The court held that where a landlord leases part of his property for a particular business, he must not derogate from his grant, i.e. he must not do anything which would render those premises unfit for the purpose for which they were leased. In this case, the plaintiff was granted a lease containing a covenant to construct buildings in accordance with approved plans, which included windows. The plaintiff was therefore entitled, by implied grant, to the access of light through the windows during the term of the lease. The defendant's use of the wall as a party wall (which led to the local authority's demand that the windows must be blocked up) derogated from the grant of the right to open the windows and the privilege of having light come through them.

Lyme Valley Squash Club Ltd v Newcastle under Lyme BC (1985)

The plaintiff company bought land from the defendant local authority for development as a squash club. The land, at the time, was surrounded on three sides by the local authority's land which was used as a public car park. The conveyance contained no express grant of a right to light. In fact, the agreement for sale had included a clause preventing the plaintiff from acquiring any easements or other rights, but this clause had been omitted from the conveyance by mistake. After the opening of the squash club, the local authority decided to build a retail store on land next to the club. The plaintiff began an action claiming that the proposed building would interfere with the access of light to the club and sought an injunction preventing the development. It claimed that it was entitled to a right to light on the basis either of the doctrine of non-derogation from grant or on the basis of section 62 of LPA 1925.

The judge held that the plaintiff was entitled to a right to light on the basis of the principle of non-derogation from grant. He decided, on the basis of correspondence and evidence from witnesses, that the parties had proceeded on the basis that the car park was a permanent feature and with the mutual intention that the plaintiff should have light to its windows. He also relied on the fact that the plaintiff owned only about one metre of land around the squash club. The judge rejected the defendant's argument that the conveyance should be rectified to include the omitted clause. He also decided that the plaintiff had acquired a right to light under section 62 of LPA 1925 (see 2.3.3 below).

However, the principle that a grantor may not derogate from his grant does not mean that rights to light will be implied which are inconsistent with the parties' intention to be implied from the circumstances existing at the time of the grant and known to the purchaser/lessee.

Birmingham, Dudley and District Banking Co v Ross (1888)

The Corporation of Birmingham granted a lease to the plaintiffs of land on which stood a newly constructed building 'with the rights, members, and appurtenants to the said premises belonging'. The building abutted a passage 20 ft wide, which the Corporation agreed to keep open and, on the other side of the passage, were buildings about 25 ft high. The Corporation then leased the land on the other side of the passage to the defendant, who pulled down the old buildings and constructed a new building which was 80 ft high. All the land was part of a larger building scheme laid out by the Corporation for the improvement of the town. The plaintiff brought an action for a mandatory injunction ordering the defendant to pull down the part of its building which interfered with its right to lights and also an injunction preventing the defendant from constructing his building so as to interfere with the plaintiff's rights to light. The plaintiff argued that there had been an express grant of a right to light, alternatively that such a right should be implied into the lease.

The Court of Appeal held that the lease contained no express right to light. It held that the extent of the light to which the plaintiff was entitled by implied grant must be measured by the circumstances which existed and were known to the parties at the time the lease was made. As the plaintiffs knew that the whole area was to be built on by the Corporation, subject only to a requirement negotiated between the parties that there should be a distance of 20 ft from the plaintiff's land, the plaintiff had no right to light beyond the protection given by the 20 ft passageway. Given the circumstances, there was no derogation from the grant. The plaintiff was not therefore entitled to an injunction.

Myers v Catterson (1889)

A railway company sold a house and land to the plaintiff. The house had been built close to the railway line and two of the windows in the plaintiff's house received some light through two of the railway arches on the railway line. The conveyance to the plaintiff stated that the land retained by the railway company would be required for constructing the railway and it contained no express words granting the plaintiff a right to light. A few years later, the railway company sold the land opposite the plaintiff's house and leased the railway arches to a third party. The defendant bought the land opposite and the lease from the third party and blocked the arches with hoardings. The plaintiff brought an action against the defendant arguing that the hoardings substantially obstructed the light to his windows and claimed a mandatory injunction requiring the defendant to take down the hoardings.

The Court of Appeal held that the vendor of one part of a property with a house on it has an implied obligation not to interfere with the light to the house sold. This was based on the principle that a grantor cannot derogate from his grant, but that he is bound to allow the premises sold to be enjoyed so far as they reasonably can be. However, in order to determine the extent of the vendor's implied obligation, it held that a court must look at the reason for the obligation and the surrounding circumstances. The surrounding circumstances showed that the obligation not to interfere with the plaintiff's light was limited in that the railway company was entitled to do anything required for the construction of its railway. Nonetheless, the hoardings had not been erected by the defendant for the purpose of the railway and he was therefore not entitled to interfere with the plaintiff's light in this way.

2.3.2 The rule in *Wheeldon v Burrows*

The 'rule in *Wheeldon v Burrows*' applies where the owner of land grants part of it (plot A) to another and retains the remainder (plot B). The rule is that, by implication, he also grants easements (including rights to light) which are necessary for the reasonable enjoyment of the property granted and which have been and are at the time of the grant used by the owners of the whole property for the benefit of the part granted. This rule is based on the principle that a grantor may not derogate from his grant (see 2.3.1 above). It operates when land is transferred, whether by sale, lease or otherwise. There is no need for a right to light previously to have been acquired (e.g. by prescription) in order for it to be impliedly granted under this rule: it is sufficient that there was a building on the part of the property sold which benefited from light from the remainder of the property.

Wheeldon v Burrows (1879)

This case concerned whether rights to light had been impliedly reserved by the vendor for the benefit of the land retained (see 2.4.1 below), not whether there had been an implied grant to a purchaser on a sale of land. However, Thesiger LJ in the Court of Appeal set out two general rules: one relating to implied grants and one to implied reservations. His rule in relation to implied grants has become known as 'the rule in *Wheeldon v Burrows*'. He stated the rule in these terms:

> 'on the grant by the owner of a tenement of part of that tenement as it is then used and enjoyed, there will pass to the grantee all those continuous and apparent easements (by which, of course, I mean quasi easements), or, in other words, all those easements which are necessary to the reasonable enjoyment of the property granted, and which have been and are at the time for the grant used by the owners of the entirety for the benefit of the part granted.'

Where a vendor sub-divides his property into two plots and simultaneously transfers both plots to new owners (instead of the vendor retaining one of the plots for himself), the new owners each obtain by implied grant the same rights for their plot as they would have obtained if the vendor had retained one plot.

Russell v Watts (1884)

Summarising the law, Fry LJ said:

> 'As the same vendor is selling to two persons at the same time, each purchaser is entitled, in favour of the house he buys, to the benefit of the maxim that no man shall derogate from his own grant but, at the same time, he has the burden of the same maxim in favour of his neighbour's

house; and the result is, that all the *quasi* easements which existed between the two lots in the hands of the one owner, the vendor, are perpetuated by way of implied grant, in the hands of the respective purchasers.'

2.3.3 Section 62 of the Law of Property Act 1925

Rights to light can also be created under section 62 of LPA 1925. Section 62 inserts words into a conveyance so that the parties do not have to set out in detail all of the rights and benefits intended to pass under the conveyance. Section 62 provides that:

> 'A conveyance of land shall be deemed to include and shall by virtue of this Act operate to convey, with the land, all ... easements, rights and advantages whatsoever, appertaining or reputed to appertain to the land or any part thereof, or, at the time of conveyance, demised, occupied, or enjoyed with or reputed or known as part or parcel of or appurtenant to the land or any part thereof.'

In relation to rights to light, section 62 operates in a very similar way to the rule in *Wheeldon v Burrows* (see 2.3.2 above). As can be seen from some of the older cases, before the enactment of section 62, a similar provision was found in section 6 of the *Conveyancing Act* 1881.

It should be noted that commentators and judges have sometimes considered a grant under section 62 as a form of express, rather than implied, grant. It makes no practical difference whether the terminology of express or implied grant is used.

The typical situation in which section 62 applies is where the owner of land sells part of it (plot A) to a purchaser and retains the remainder (plot B). If there is a house on plot A, which enjoyed light from plot B prior to the sale, a right to light passes to the purchaser on the sale as a result of section 62 without the need for any express grant of a right to light in the conveyance.

Lyme Valley Squash Club Ltd v Newcastle under Lyme BC (1985)

The plaintiff company bought land from the defendant local authority for development as a squash club. The land, at the time, was surrounded on three sides by the local authority's land which was used as a public car park. The conveyance contained no express grant of a right to light. In fact, the agreement for sale had included a clause preventing the plaintiff from acquiring any easements or other rights, but this clause had been omitted from the conveyance by mistake. After the sale and opening of the squash club, the local authority decided to build a retail store on land next to the club. The plaintiff began an action claiming that the proposed building would interfere with the access of light to the club and sought an injunction preventing the development. It claimed that it was entitled to a right to light on the basis either of the doctrine of non-derogation from grant or on the basis of section 62 of LPA 1925.

The judge held that the plaintiff was entitled to a right to light on the basis of the principle of non-derogation from grant (see 2.3.1 above). In relation to section 62, he stated that this section implied general words into a conveyance so that the conveyance to the club included an easement of light to its windows similar to the right which was actually being enjoyed at the time of the conveyance. Although the agreement for sale pre-dated the construction of the squash club, by the time that the conveyance was sealed, the club had been completed and the windows were enjoying the access of light over the car park. Therefore, the plaintiff had acquired a right to light under section 62 of LPA 1925.

Section 62(4) of LPA 1925 provides that the section only operates to grant a right to light if a contrary intention is not expressed in the conveyance.

Broomfield v Williams (1897)

The defendant owned two adjoining plots. He sold one plot to the plaintiff, on which there was a house with windows overlooking the other plot, which he retained. No express right to light was granted in the conveyance. The conveyance described the retained land as 'building land', but contained no express reservation to the defendant of any right to build on that land. The defendant then built a house on the retained land and the plaintiff brought proceedings against him claiming that the new house interfered with the access of light to the plaintiff's windows. The plaintiff relied on section 6 of the *Conveyancing Act* 1881 (the predecessor to section 62 of LPA 1925) and the principle of non-derogation from grant. The defendant argued that because the retained land was described as 'building land' in the conveyance, there was no limit on his right to build on the land and that this showed a contrary intention in accordance with section 6(4) of the *Conveyancing Act* 1881.

The Court of Appeal held that the reference in the conveyance to the defendant's retained land as 'building land' was not enough to show that the parties had not intended the right to light to pass under the Act because it was quite possible to build on the adjoining land without obstructing the windows of the plaintiff's house. The Court of Appeal also relied on the principle that a grantor could not derogate from his own grant, stating that the defendant could not build on his own land in such a way as to block out the plaintiff's light altogether, as this would frustrate the very object of the grant.

Section 62 of LPA 1925 cannot operate to transfer a right to light to a purchaser by implication unless the vendor would have been entitled expressly to grant him a right to light.

Quicke v Chapman (1903)

The defendant builder entered into an agreement with the Ecclesiastical Commissioners which entitled him to build houses on the Commissioners' land. The parties agreed that, once each house constructed by the defendant was completed to the Commissioners' satisfaction, they would grant him a lease of that plot for 99 years. The defendant constructed a house (no. 28) on one of the plots and the Commissioners granted him a lease of that plot in the agreed form. The defendant transferred the lease of no. 28 to the plaintiffs. On the adjoining plot, the defendant then started to construct another house (no. 30) in accordance with plans approved by the Commissioners. When no. 30 was completed, the plaintiffs found that the house obstructed the light to their house and therefore brought an action against the defendant claiming an injunction and damages. The plaintiffs argued that they were entitled to a right to light by implied grant, relying on section 6 of the *Conveyancing Act* 1881 (the predecessor to section 62 of LPA 1925) and the principle of non-derogation from grant.

The Court of Appeal held that the plaintiffs had not been granted a right to light under the Act. The rights that passed under section 6 were limited to those rights which the vendor could have granted expressly. The defendant did not have the power to make an express grant of a right to light because, at the time he sold no. 28 to the plaintiffs, he did not have a lease of no. 30. At most, he was a licensee and, therefore, did not have a sufficient proprietary interest in no. 30 to make an express grant of a right to light. Consequently, no grant of a right to light could be implied under the Act.

2.3.4 Easements of necessity

Some easements can be impliedly granted on the basis that they are necessary to the grant of the property. They are known as easements of necessity. It is thought that rights to light cannot be easements of necessity, because they are not rights without which the property cannot be enjoyed at all, but they are merely necessary for the reasonable enjoyment of the property. This follows from the case of *Ray v Hazeldine* (1904) (see 2.4.2 below). Although the case was about implied reservation, not implied grant, it is considered that the reasoning applies equally to implied grants of rights to light.

2.4 ACQUISITION BY IMPLIED RESERVATION

2.4.1 The general rule

It is less likely that a court will decide that a right to light (or any easement) has been impliedly reserved than impliedly granted. If a vendor of land wishes to reserve any right, including a right to light, over the land granted (plot A) in favour of the retained land (plot B), the general rule is that he must do this expressly in clear and unambiguous terms. The reason for this is the principle that a vendor shall not derogate from his own grant (see 2.3.1 above). This general rule was the second of two general rules set out by the Court of Appeal in the case of *Wheeldon v Burrows* (1879).

Wheeldon v Burrows (1879)

Mr Tetley owned and occupied a piece of land and an adjoining workshop. The workshop windows enjoyed access to light over the piece of land. Mr Tetley sold the piece of land at auction and made no express reservation in the conveyance that the workshop should continue to enjoy access to light over the land sold. The land was subsequently re-sold to the plaintiff. Shortly afterwards, Mr Tetley sold the workshop to the defendant. The plaintiff erected hoardings on her land which blocked the light to the workshop windows and the defendant pulled the hoardings down. The plaintiff commenced proceedings against the defendant to prevent him from trespassing on her land in order to pull down the hoardings. The defendant argued that the trespass was justified because he was exercising his right to prevent any obstruction to his rights to light. The defendant argued that, although the conveyance of the piece of land contained no express reservation of a right to light, there was an implied reservation of such a right. The judge rejected the defendant's argument and awarded the plaintiff an injunction restraining any further trespass. The defendant appealed.

The Court of Appeal dismissed the defendant's appeal and held that, because Mr Tetley had not expressly reserved a right to the access of light for the workshop when he sold the land to the plaintiff, the defendant (who had subsequently bought the workshop from Mr Tetley) had no such right. The plaintiff was therefore free to build on her land as she pleased. Thesiger LJ held that there were two general rules in relation to implication of rights on a sale. The first rule related to implied grants (see 2.3.2 above). The second rule was that, if the vendor intended to reserve any right over the land sold, it was his duty to reserve it expressly in the conveyance. Both rules were based on the maxim that a grantor should not derogate from his grant. He said that the second rule was subject to exceptions, one of which was for easements of necessity. However, in this case, the second rule applied and there was no implied reservation of a right to light for the workshop.

2.4.2 Exceptions to the general rule

There can be exceptions to the general rule that the reservation of a right must be expressly set out. The most common exception is for easements of necessity. However, it is considered that rights to light do not fall within the category of easements of necessity. This is because they are not easements without which the property cannot be enjoyed at all, but they are merely necessary for the reasonable enjoyment of the property.

Ray v Hazeldine (1904)

The defendant owned two adjoining properties. He sold one to the plaintiff's predecessor and retained the other, without expressly reserving any rights over the property sold for the benefit of the property retained. Subsequently, the plaintiff built a wall on her premises which blocked out the light to two windows in the defendant's premises. One of the windows had provided light to a pantry, which (after the obstruction) was useless as a pantry. The defendant knocked down the wall and the plaintiff began an action for a declaration that she was entitled to build on her premises so as to obstruct the defendant's light. The defendant argued that the light to the two windows was absolutely necessary for the use and enjoyment of that part of the house and, therefore, that there was an implied easement of necessity reserved in the conveyance to the plaintiff's predecessor.

The judge held, relying on *Wheeldon v Burrows*, that the general rule was that if a vendor of land wished to reserve a right for the benefit of the retained land, he must do it by express words in the deed of conveyance. He accepted that there was an exception for easements of necessity, but held that there was a distinction between what was absolutely necessary and what was reasonably required for the enjoyment of the land or building as it stood. He found that the light, including that to the pantry, did not fall into the category of necessity. He therefore made a declaration that the plaintiff was entitled to build on her property in such manner as to obstruct the light to the two windows.

3
Acquisition by prescription

3.1 METHODS OF PRESCRIPTION

Where a right to light has not been acquired by grant or reservation (see Chapter 2), it can be acquired by prescription. There are three methods of acquiring a right to light by prescription:

- at common law;
- by lost modern grant; or
- under the *Prescription Act* 1832.

As set out in the following paragraphs, different criteria apply to each method of acquisition. For reasons explained below, claims for common law prescription are unlikely to succeed. However, there are circumstances in which a claim will fail under the doctrine of lost modern grant, but will succeed under the *Prescription Act* and vice versa. These issues make the law complex and confusing.

In order to ensure the best chance of success in litigation, parties frequently rely on all three methods as alternatives. In *Tehidy Minerals Ltd v Norman* (1971) (see 4.4 below) the Court of Appeal expressed its view that it was no longer desirable or necessary to have three different methods by which prescriptive rights could be acquired and that the legislature should intervene to simplify this area of law. However, as yet, no such intervention has taken place and the law in this area remains unnecessarily overcomplicated (see also 1.6 above).

3.1.1 A right to light cannot be acquired by prescription for a vacant piece of land

A right to light cannot be acquired by any of the three methods of prescription for a vacant piece of land. The *Prescription Act* specifically states that the right to light has to be acquired in relation to a building (see 3.4.1 and 3.4.2 below).

Roberts v Macord (1832)

The plaintiff and defendant owned adjoining pieces of land. The defendant's land included a timber yard and saw-pit. The plaintiff constructed a wall on his land, which the defendant pulled down, claiming that it obstructed the light and air to his timber yard and saw-pit. The plaintiff brought an action against the defendant in trespass. The judge rejected the defendant's argument that he had acquired a right to light and air by prescription, stating that this would mean that a man would be entitled to acquire an exclusive right to the light and air merely by laying a few boards on the ground to dry. This was not sufficient to raise the presumption of a grant of a right to light and air.

Potts v Smith (1868)

The plaintiff leased a property adjacent to the defendant's land. The defendant then built on his land and the plaintiff claimed that the new building interfered with the free access of light and air to the house and the garden. In relation to the garden, the judge held that a right to light and air over open ground could not be acquired by prescription. If such a right were allowed in favour of open land, the consequence would be that no-one would ever be able to build to the edge of his own land. The judge, relying on *Roberts v Macord*, went on to say that:

> 'in the present case, and in all others, it must be well understood that, however agreeable and beautiful a garden may be, if another person has land immediately adjoining it, neither the pleasure derived from the scent or sight of the flowers will prevent the owner of the adjoining land from erecting whatever buildings on his land he thinks fit.'

3.2 PRESCRIPTION AT COMMON LAW

A right to light can be acquired by prescription at common law where the property has enjoyed the access of light 'as of right', since time immemorial. There are three key criteria in relation to a claim for prescription at common law:

- the light must have been enjoyed since time immemorial;
- the light must have been enjoyed 'as of right'; and
- a right to light can only be acquired by and against freehold owners of property.

3.2.1 Enjoyment since time immemorial

Prescription at common law requires the claimant to prove that his building has enjoyed the access of light over the servient land since 'time immemorial'. This is sometimes called the period of legal memory. In 1275 time immemorial was fixed as 1189, the first year of the reign of Richard I. At that time, the prescription period was some 86 years. However, the date has never since been altered. These days, except for a very small number of ancient buildings, it will not be possible to prove that light has been enjoyed since 1189.

In the absence of proof to the contrary, however, the courts will accept that evidence of enjoyment of a right to light for so long as anyone can remember is sufficient to acquire a right to light by prescription at common law.

Aynsley v Glover (1875)

The plaintiff owned an inn, incorporating buildings which had previously been cottages. Some of the inn's windows received light over the defendant's adjoining land. The defendant then proposed building on his land and the plaintiff brought an action against him claiming an injunction to prevent him building in a way which would interfere with the inn's rights to light. The plaintiff claimed that he had acquired rights to light at common law and under the *Prescription Act*. The plaintiff was awarded an injunction and the defendant appealed.

The appeal was dismissed. The appeal court held that the plaintiff had established a right to light since time immemorial. A man of over 80 years old had given evidence that the windows had been there as long as he could remember. There was also evidence that the cottages were in existence in 1808 from a deed dated that year. There was no evidence of when the cottages had actually been built. Although there was evidence of common possession of the plaintiff's and defendant's properties at one stage, there was no evidence of common ownership. The court therefore held that there was proof that the windows had existed as far back as living memory went, showing a right to light from time immemorial.

Since a right to light acquired by common law prescription is based on the presumption that it has been enjoyed since 1189, a defendant can defeat a claim where he can show that the dominant property was actually built after 1189. A claim can also be defeated by showing that at some point since 1189 and the present day the dominant and servient properties have been owned by the same person.

Wheaton v Maple & Co (1893)

The plaintiff built two houses on his land in 1852. The defendants, who leased the adjacent land from the Crown, then constructed new buildings on that land and obstructed the light to the plaintiff's houses. The plaintiff claimed that he had acquired rights to light by common law prescription, lost modern grant and under the *Prescription Act*. The Court of Appeal quickly disposed of the claim for common law prescription on the basis that enjoyment from time immemorial could not be presumed when it was admitted that the houses had only come into existence in 1852.

Bowring Services Ltd v Scottish Widows' Fund & Life Assurance Society (1995)

The plaintiff had a long leasehold interest in a building which received light over an adjoining site owned by the defendant. The defendant started to construct buildings on its site in a way which the plaintiff claimed would interfere with its light. The plaintiff brought proceedings against the defendant, claiming that its property had acquired a right to light by common law prescription, lost modern grant and under the *Prescription Act*. The defendant applied to strike out the plaintiff's claim as an abuse of process.

The judge allowed the defendant's application and struck out the plaintiff's claim. In relation to common law prescription, he stated that the difficulty of proving enjoyment since 1189 had been alleviated by the courts holding that evidence of enjoyment for as long as anyone could remember raised a presumption that such enjoyment had existed for the period of legal memory. However, in this case, as it was not disputed that the plaintiff's property had not been built until the 1960s, he held that no claim could succeed for common law prescription.

3.2.2 The enjoyment must be 'as of right'

For both common law prescription and the doctrine of lost modern grant (see 3.3 below), the enjoyment of the light must be 'as of right'. This topic is dealt with in the section on lost modern grant (at 3.3.3 below).

3.2.3 By and against whom can the right to light be claimed?

A right to light acquired by common law prescription can only operate by and against freehold owners. This is also the position under the doctrine of lost modern grant (see 3.3.4 below), but differs from the position under the *Prescription Act* where the right can also be claimed by and against a leaseholder (see 3.4.7 below).

Wheaton v Maple & Co (1893)

The plaintiff built two houses on his land in 1852. The defendants, who leased the adjacent land from the Crown, then constructed new buildings on that land and obstructed the light to the plaintiff's houses. The plaintiff claimed that he had acquired rights of light by common law prescription, lost modern grant and under the *Prescription Act* against the defendant lessees. The Court of Appeal held that rights could only be acquired by prescription at common law by or against freehold owners.

3.3 LOST MODERN GRANT

3.3.1 General principles

The doctrine of lost modern grant was developed by the courts in the 17th and 18th centuries so that easements could be acquired without having to satisfy the virtually impossible requirement of common law prescription, namely enjoyment since 1189. The doctrine relies on a fiction that, if 20 years' enjoyment can be shown without interruption, a grant has been made which has now been lost.

The key elements of lost modern grant are:

- a fictitious grant is presumed if 20 years' uninterrupted enjoyment can be shown;
- the light must have been enjoyed 'as of right'; and
- a right to light can only be acquired by and against freehold owners of property.

3.3.2 Fiction of a grant after 20 years' enjoyment

Once 20 years' user has been established, a fictitious grant is presumed. As the doctrine is based on the fiction of a grant, the fact that there was no actual grant does not matter, unless such a grant would have been legally impossible (see below). This was made clear by the Court of Appeal in *Tehidy Minerals Ltd v Norman* (1971), interpreting the House of Lords' decision in *Dalton v Angus* (1881). Buckley LJ in *Tehidy* stated:

> 'where there has been upwards of 20 years' uninterrupted enjoyment of an easement, such enjoyment having the necessary qualities to fulfil the requirements of prescription, then unless, for some reason such as incapacity on the part of the person or person who might at some time before the commencement of the 20-year period have made a grant, the existence of such a grant is impossible, the law will adopt a legal fiction that such a grant was made, in spite of any direct evidence that no such grant was in fact made.'

Examples of circumstances in which the courts will not adopt the legal fiction that a grant was made because an actual grant would have been impossible include where:

- the Custom of London applies; and
- the presumed grantor is incapable of making a grant at all or doing so without the approval of another party.

3.3.2.1 The Custom of London

The Custom of London gives the right to freeholders within the City of London to build a new building on ancient foundations to whatever height they please, regardless of whether it interferes with ancient lights or windows in neighbouring properties. A claim for a right to light under the *Prescription Act* will be unaffected by the Custom of London, as section 3 of the Act applies notwithstanding any local usage or custom to the contrary (see 3.4.1 below). However, a claim based on lost modern grant or common law prescription will fail if the Custom of London applies.

Perry v Eames (1891)

The plaintiffs claimed rights to light over the site of the old Bankruptcy Court in the City of London. The judge held that no right to light could be acquired under the *Prescription Act* because the site was owned by the Crown and the Act did not apply to the Crown (see 3.4.7 below). The plaintiffs claimed, in the alternative, that a right had been acquired by lost modern grant or by prescription at common law before the site had been purchased by the Crown. The judge held that the site was part of the ancient Cloth Market to which the Custom of London applied. This meant that a man might rebuild on ancient foundations to whatever height he pleased, even if neighbours' windows were obstructed, if there were no written agreement to the contrary. Therefore, although the Custom of London would not apply to a claim under the *Prescription Act* as a result of the wording of section 3 (which stated that the right was acquired notwithstanding customs to the contrary), it did apply to claims for prescription at common law and under the doctrine of lost modern grant and meant that no rights could be acquired by these methods of prescription.

Bowring Services Ltd v Scottish Widows' Fund & Life Assurance Society (1995)

The plaintiff had a long leasehold interest in a building which received light over an adjoining site owned by the defendant. Both properties were in the City of London. The defendant started to construct buildings on its site in a way which the plaintiff claimed would interfere with its light. The plaintiff brought proceedings against the defendant claiming that its property had acquired a right to light by common law prescription, lost modern grant and under the *Prescription Act*. The defendant applied to strike out the plaintiff's claim as an abuse of process.

The judge allowed the defendant's application and struck out the plaintiff's claim. The judge held that the claim based on lost modern grant failed because of the Custom of London, which entitled the defendant to rebuild his property on ancient foundations to whatever height he pleased, even though it interfered with the plaintiff's light.

3.3.2.2 Presumed grantor incapable of making grant

Where the presumed grantor would have been incapable of making a grant or would have been unable to make a grant without the approval of a third party, the court will not presume that a grant was made. Examples of situations in which the court has refused to presume that a grant was made have occurred in claims for rights of way, but such issues could also arise in claims for rights to light.

Oakley v Boston (1976)

The plaintiffs were the owners of property known as the Old Rectory, which had previously been glebe land and vested in the rector of the parish. The plaintiffs began an action for trespass against the defendant, who claimed that he had a right of way over the land on the basis of lost modern grant, (i.e. on the basis of a presumed grant by the rector) and under the *Prescription Act*. The Court of Appeal held that the rector could only have granted a right of way with the approval of the Ecclesiastical Commissioners. The doctrine of lost modern grant arose where the servient owner, with knowledge of the exercise of the right of way, acquiesced in this so that his consent by way of a deed could be presumed. However, the court held that the doctrine could not be extended to allow it to presume that the Commissioners, carrying out their statutory duty, would have approved of the grant. There was no evidence that the Commissioners knew of, or had acquiesced in, the use of the way.

3.3.2.3 The 20-year period need not be immediately before the action

A right to light can be established under the doctrine of lost modern grant if 20 years' use and enjoyment can be established. Unlike a claim under the *Prescription Act* (see 3.4.3 below), the 20-year period does not need to be immediately before the commencement of the action. This means that, in some cases, a claim under the doctrine of lost modern grant will succeed where a claim under the *Prescription Act* will fail.

Marine & General Mutual Life Assurance Society v St James' Real Estate Co Ltd (1991)

The plaintiff claimed damages for interference with its rights to light as a result of a proposed redevelopment of the defendant's adjacent property. The claim was made under the *Prescription Act* and the doctrine of lost modern grant. The claim under the Act failed because the windows had been blocked in and the light had not been enjoyed for the period of 20 years immediately before the action. The claim for lost modern grant, however, succeeded because the right had been enjoyed for 20 years before the windows had been blocked in. The judge rejected the defendant's argument that the right had been abandoned by blocking in of the windows (see Chapter 4 for abandonment).

3.3.3 The enjoyment must be 'as of right'

To acquire a right to light by common law prescription or under the doctrine of lost modern grant, the light must have been enjoyed 'as of right'. In order to satisfy this test, the light must be enjoyed by the claimant:

- without the use of force;

- openly; and
- without permission.

In the older cases, this is often described by the Latin phrase '*nec vi, nec clam, nec precario*' (not by force, not secretly, not with permission). A useful summary of the general principles is set out in the Court of Appeal judgment in *Sturges v Bridgman* (1879), which concerned a dispute about noise.

Few rights to light cases have dealt with the question of whether the right has been enjoyed as of right. The cases in this section therefore relate to the acquisition of other easements, including rights of way. However, they set out the general principles.

Sturges v Bridgman (1879)

Thesiger LJ stated, when giving the judgment of the Court of Appeal:

> 'Consent or acquiescence of the owner of the servient tenement lies at the root of prescription, and of the fiction of a lost grant, and hence the acts or user, which go to the proof of either the one or the other, must be, in the language of the civil law, *nec vi, nec clam, nec precario*; for a man cannot, as a general rule, be said to consent to or acquiesce in the acquisition by his neighbour of an easement through an enjoyment of which he has no knowledge, actual or constructive, or which he contests and endeavours to interrupt, or which he temporarily licences.'

As set out in *Sturges v Bridgman*, consent to or acquiescence in the enjoyment, with knowledge of it, are necessary elements of a claim to use as of right. Some of the older cases appeared to suggest that tolerance of the dominant owner's usage could prevent acquisition by prescription as it would not be as of right. It has now been established that tolerance does not prevent the acquisition of a right.

Mills v Silver (1991)

This case concerned a claim of a right of way under the doctrine of lost modern grant. However, the principles are relevant to the acquisition of rights to light.

In 1985 the first and second defendants purchased a hill farm adjoining the plaintiff's farm land. The only vehicular access to the defendants' farm from the public highway was over a track on the plaintiff's land. Shortly after the purchase, the first and second defendants employed the third defendant, a contractor, to construct a stone road along the track to make it possible for use in all types of weather. The plaintiff sought an injunction to prevent the first and second defendants from using the track for vehicular access and against all three defendants for damages for trespass. It was argued that the right of way had not been used as of right since the servient owner had tolerated the user of the track for vehicles, out of good neighbourliness and because the use was too insignificant to matter. The judge held that the defendants had failed to establish a prescriptive right to use the track. One of the grounds on which the plaintiffs' claim failed was that tolerance of the use of the track was fatal to the claim. The defendants appealed.

The Court of Appeal allowed the appeal. It held that a prescriptive right arises where there has been user as of right in which the servient owner has, with the necessary degree of knowledge, acquiesced. Therefore mere acquiescence in, or tolerance of, the use by the servient owner could not prevent the user being as of right. There was no justification for drawing a distinction between the words 'acquiescence' (which did not prevent a prescriptive right arising) and 'tolerance' or 'toleration' (which it was argued did prevent a right arising): the words had broadly the same meaning. The defendants had therefore established the prescriptive right of way that they claimed.

Where the owners of the dominant property are under the mistaken belief that the servient owner has granted an express right to light, this will not prevent enjoyment being as of right. However, where both dominant and servient owners act on a mistaken assumption that there is an express right, this will prevent enjoyment of the easement being as of right.

Bridle v Ruby (1989)

The plaintiff (the owner of no. 13) and his predecessor mistakenly believed that the conveyance of no. 13 expressly contained a right of way over the driveway of no. 12 and had used the right of way for 22 years under this mistaken belief. In fact, a clause providing for such a right of way had been deleted in the final draft of the conveyance of no. 13, so that there was no such express right. The plaintiff claimed a right of way on the basis (among others) of lost modern grant. The defendant argued that an easement could not be acquired by a party by prescription on the basis of a mistaken view as to his rights.

The Court of Appeal held that asserting a right in the mistaken belief that it is an express right does not negative a claim by prescription, whether at common law, by lost modern grant or under the *Prescription Act*. The requirement that user is as of right means that the owner of the servient land is given sufficient opportunity of knowing that the plaintiff is, by his conduct, asserting the right to do what he is doing without the owner's permission. It does not prevent the plaintiff acquiring a right because he is mistaken as to his rights. In this case, there was no trace of temporary permission or a series of temporary permissions to prevent the enjoyment being as of right.

Chamber Colliery Company v Hopwood (1886)

The defendants leased the coal mines under their property to the plaintiffs for 50 years. The latter constructed a drain, with the knowledge of the defendants' agent, which took water to other land owned by the plaintiffs on which they built reservoirs. At the end of the lease, the defendants blocked up the drain. The plaintiffs started proceedings, claiming a right by prescription to the drainage of water to their other land, but the defendants argued that the drain had not been enjoyed as of right. The Court of Appeal decided that the right was not enjoyed as of right for two reasons. First, the defendants had assumed that the plaintiffs were entitled to the right under the lease and the plaintiffs had acquiesced in that assumption. Secondly, the enjoyment had been on the basis of business friendship or indulgence. In neither case, did the enjoyment last beyond the end of the lease and it was not as of right.

Once a right to light is obstructed or objected to, it will not be used as of right. If the dominant owner forcibly removes the obstruction, the enjoyment will be by force and not as of right.

Newnham v Willison (1988)

This case concerned a claim for a vehicular right of way by the plaintiff and whether the right of way included a 'swept curve' or merely a sharp angled turn. The defendants had objected to the right of way by putting down various obstructions, including concrete boulders, footings and poles and ultimately a fence. Some of the obstructions (although not the fence) were removed by the plaintiff. The issue was whether the user was as of right or by force. The Court of Appeal held that user by force occurs once the dominant owner knows that his user is being objected to and has become contentious. If the dominant owner then physically overcomes the objections, such as by removing an obstruction, there is sufficient evidence to show that the use is no longer as of right. The court held that, in this case, it was perfectly clear that the defendants were objecting to the swept turn and therefore that the user was not as of right.

Smith v Brudenell-Bruce (2002)

This case also concerned a claim to a right of way by the claimant. From 1975, when the claimant bought his cottage, he used a track over the defendant's land. In September and October 1998, the defendants wrote to the claimant prohibiting him from using the track. In 2000 the claimant brought an action against the defendant claiming a right of way. The judge held that the claim under the *Prescription Act* failed because the claimant's use of the track ceased to be as of right in October 1998. (Enjoyment of rights of way, unlike rights to light, must be as of right in order to succeed under the *Prescription Act*.)

3.3.4 By and against whom can a presumption of lost modern grant be made?

As with common law prescription (see 3.2.3 above), a presumption of lost modern grant can only be made by and against freeholders of the dominant and servient property.

Simmons v Dobson (1991)

The defendants and plaintiff were lessees of two properties owned by the same freeholder owner. The defendants blocked a passageway which the plaintiff used to reach the road. The plaintiff therefore brought an action claiming a right of way over the passageway on the basis, amongst others, of lost modern grant. The Court of Appeal held that the common law rule that rights could only be acquired by prescription by and against freehold owners also applied to the doctrine of lost modern grant.

3.4 PRESCRIPTION ACT 1832

3.4.1 General principles

The *Prescription Act* 1832 is called an 'Act for shortening the time of prescription in certain cases'. The preamble, now repealed, to the Act explained that it was intended to remedy the problem caused by the need to establish enjoyment since time immemorial before an easement could be acquired by prescription. However, by 1832, the courts had already introduced the doctrine of lost modern grant, which also sought to remedy this problem (see 3.3.1 above). Although this may not have been the original intention of those drafting the Act, claimants now often rely on all three methods of prescription to claim a right to light.

The *Prescription Act* introduced its own problems and its wording is far from straightforward. In the words of the judge in the case of *Smith v Brudenell-Bruce* (2002), it is remarkable that in the 21st century a central part of the law relating to property is still to be found in a statute of 1832 whose drafting has been criticised repeatedly.

Two sections of the Act are relevant to the acquisition of a right to light:

- section 3 sets out the criteria for the acquisition of the right; and
- section 4 is relevant to the calculation of the 20-year period necessary for the acquisition of the right.

> '**Section 3: Right to the use of light enjoyed for twenty years, indefeasible, unless shown to have been by consent**
>
> . . . When the access and use of light to and for any dwelling house, workshop, or other building shall have been actually enjoyed therewith for the full period of twenty years without interruption, the right thereto shall be deemed absolute and indefeasible, any local usage or custom to the contrary notwithstanding, unless it shall appear that the same was enjoyed by some consent or agreement expressly made or given for that purpose by deed or writing.'
>
> '**Section 4: Before mentioned periods to be deemed those next before suits for claiming to which such periods relate – What shall constitute an interruption**
>
> . . . Each of the respective periods of years herein-before mentioned shall be deemed and taken to be the period next before some suit or action wherein the claim or matter to which such period may relate shall have been or shall be brought into question; and ... no act or other matter shall be deemed to be an interruption, within the meaning of this statute, unless the same shall have been or shall be submitted to or acquiesced in for one year after the party interrupted shall have had or shall have notice thereof, and of the person making or authorizing the same to be made.'

In summary, the Act provides that a right to light will be acquired under section 3 where:

- A dwelling house, workshop or other building
- For a 20-year period before commencement of the action
- Has actually enjoyed light
- Without interruption
- Unless it has been enjoyed by written consent or agreement.

In addition, case law has established that a right to light can be acquired by or against freehold or leasehold owners but that it cannot be acquired against the Crown.

If the claimant satisfies all the hurdles set out above, the dominant property acquires an 'absolute and indefeasible' right to light.

3.4.2 A dwelling house, workshop or other building

Section 3 provides that the light must be enjoyed by a dwelling house, workshop or other building for the 20-year period. This has raised a number of issues:

- the stage of construction at which a property begins to enjoy light;
- which buildings, other than houses and workshops, are capable of acquiring rights to light; and
- the need for light to be enjoyed by defined apertures in a building.

3.4.2.1 Stage of construction of property

It is not necessary for a property to be completely fit for habitation before it can begin to enjoy light for the purposes of starting the 20-year period in section 3 of the *Prescription Act*. It will enjoy light for the purposes of the Act from the date when the basic structural elements have been completed and the window apertures installed, even if internal works are not complete and the window panes have not yet been put in.

Courtauld v Legh (1869)

The plaintiff and defendant owned adjoining properties. By 1830, the plaintiff's predecessor had built a house to the stage at which all structural parts had been completed, the roof was finished, the floors laid and windows installed. However, the internal fitting out and decoration were not completed and, in that sense, the house was unfit for habitation. In 1852, the plaintiff bought it, completed it and lived there for two years, after which time it remained empty. In 1865, the defendant extended his house, obstructing the access of light to the plaintiff's house. The issue was whether the plaintiff had acquired a right to light under the *Prescription Act*. The defendant argued that a right to light could not be acquired unless there was occupation because, without this, there would not be actual enjoyment of the light.

The court held that it was not necessary for the house to be occupied in order for light to be enjoyed. It decided that, once a house had reached the stage of having external and internal walls, roof, flooring and windows, capable of being opened and shut and admitting light, the owner could be said to enjoy and use the access of light. A right to light had therefore been acquired by 20 years' enjoyment of light before the claim was brought.

Collis v Laugher (1894)

The defendant erected a hoarding in front of and about 18 in. from two windows in the plaintiff's house, obstructing the light entering it. The plaintiff began an action, claiming a right to light under section 3 of the *Prescription Act*. The issue was whether the plaintiff's property had enjoyed a right to light for 20 years before commencement of the action. Twenty years earlier, the external walls and roof of the plaintiff's house had been built. However, at that stage, the floors were not completely laid on the joists, the gas and water were not completely connected and the window apertures had no sashes or glass in them. This work was not completed and the house was not fit for habitation until some time later.

The judge held that, despite this, the house was finished as a building 20 years before the action began because all external work was done, the walls were finished, the roof was on and tiled and the building was wind and weather tight. Following *Courtauld v Legh*, he found that it was not necessary that the building should be occupied or completely fit for habitation. The windows were openings through which light could be obtained and through which the benefit of light had been enjoyed. The plaintiff had therefore established a right to light and the judge granted an injunction preventing the defendant from interfering with this right.

3.4.2.2 Other buildings

Section 3 applies to houses, workshops or other building. The courts have not provided a definition of all structures which fall within the words 'or other building'. It is clear that not all structures will fall within this phrase. It has been decided that an open-sided structure for storing timber does not, but that an open-sided garage and a greenhouse do. A useful test set out in one case (*Smith & Co (Orpington) v Morris* (1962)) had four parts:

- whether the structure gives substantial shelter from the elements;
- whether the structure ordinarily requires light by means of windows or fixed apertures;
- whether the structure has windows; and
- whether the structure is attached to the soil in such a way as to pass under a conveyance of the land without special mention.

Harris v De Pinna (1886)

The plaintiff was a timber merchant on whose property a structure consisting of timber stages had been constructed for storing and seasoning timber and showing it to customers. This structure was permanent and consisted of several floors constructed from upright timbers fixed in stone bases. The structure was left open on the side towards the defendant's premises to admit light and air. The defendant began the erection of warehouses on his property and the plaintiff claimed that this would interfere with the access of light to his structure.

The judge held that the structure was not a building for the purposes of the *Prescription Act*. He considered that in order to fall within the words 'or other building', the building must be analogous to the buildings actually mentioned in section 3, i.e. a dwelling-house or workshop and that not every structure was a building. In reaching his decision on this structure, he took into account the nature of the construction, its design and use, that it was not enclosed, was open on three sides, had spaces that let in light rather than windows and that it could be removed at the end of the tenancy.

Overall, he considered that an ordinary man with a reasonable knowledge of the English language would not call this structure a building. The plaintiff appealed but the Court of Appeal dismissed the appeal without needing to decide whether or not the structure was a building (by deciding that light had not been enjoyed through defined apertures: see 3.4.2.3 below).

Clifford v Holt (1899)

The plaintiff had a greenhouse in his garden, one wall of which was a party wall between his property and that of the defendant. The defendant began raising the party wall to form one side of a racquet court. The plaintiff claimed an injunction to prevent the defendant increasing the height of the party wall, on the ground that this would obstruct light to his greenhouse. The defendant argued that a greenhouse was not a building within section 3 of the *Prescription Act*.

The judge did not accept that the building must be analogous to a dwelling-house or workshop, which had been the view of the judge in *Harris v De Pinna*. He did accept that not everything which was built would fall within section 3 of the *Prescription Act*. In determining whether the greenhouse was a building for the purposes of the Act, the judge considered whether the greenhouse was a building which required access of light for the ordinary purposes for which light is required. He concluded that the greenhouse was such a building and granted the plaintiff an injunction. He did not decide which other buildings would be covered by section 3, although he gave examples of chapels, studios, picture galleries and lecture rooms.

Smith & Co (Orpington) v Morris (1962)

The plaintiff owned an open-sided garage, used for housing lorries, which had seven bays. The dispute concerned a window over a bench in one of the bays. A dispute arose as to whether the plaintiff had a right to light in relation to that window.

One of the issues was whether the structure was a building for the purposes of section 3 of the *Prescription Act*. The judge in this case (like the judge in *Clifford v Holt*) did not consider that a building had to be analogous to a dwelling-house or workshop in order to fall within the phrase 'or other building'. He concluded that the main points to be considered in determining whether a structure was a building were:

(1) Did the structure give substantial shelter from the elements?

(2) Was it one which ordinarily required light by means of windows or fixed apertures?

(3) Had it got windows?

(4) Was it so attached to the soil as to pass under a conveyance of the land without special mention?

In this case, the judge decided that the answer to all these questions was 'yes' and therefore he held that the structure was a building.

3.4.2.3 The light must be received through a defined aperture

The Act provides that light must be enjoyed by a house, workshop or other building. It does not refer to windows. However, it is clear from the cases that the light must be enjoyed by a window or other aperture whose purpose is to admit light. A skylight or sloping glass roof is such an aperture. However, a door is not, unless it is wholly or partly glass.

Tapling v Jones (1865)

The Lord Chancellor, in the House of Lords, stated that section 3 of the *Prescription Act* should be read by adding in the words 'any window of' before 'any dwelling house'. This would mean that the section would read: 'When the access and use of light to and for *any window of* any dwelling-house, workshop or other building shall have been actually enjoyed therewith for the full period of twenty years without interruption, the right thereto shall be deemed absolute and indefeasible …'

Easton v Isted (1903)

In this case, the plaintiff argued that he had acquired a right to light under the *Prescription Act* in respect of a skylight or glazed roof, which had originally been part of a conservatory. The main issue was whether the light was enjoyed by virtue of a written agreement in relation to the light received through 'windows' (see 3.4.6 below). The judge held that the plaintiff's skylight would fall within section 3 of the *Prescription Act* unless the light had been enjoyed by consent or agreement in writing. However, he held that the word 'windows' in the written agreement included skylights and, therefore, that no right had been acquired under the Act. The Court of Appeal upheld the judge's decision.

Levet v Gas Light and Coke Company (1919)

The plaintiff leased a workshop with two doors, which were opened for a variety of purposes, including admitting light. He claimed a right to light over the defendant's land in relation to the doors. The judge held that section 3 of the *Prescription Act* was intended to apply to windows or apertures in the nature of windows, and not to apertures with doors in them, which were primarily constructed for the purpose of being closed and thus excluding light. He commented that, if a door could be fully or partially open at different times, it would not be possible to identify the aperture through which light had been enjoyed or how much light had been enjoyed. The plaintiff's claim for loss of light through the doors, therefore, failed.

Allen v Greenwood (1980)

This case concerned a greenhouse. The main issue was whether an extraordinary amount of light could be acquired under section 3 of the *Prescription Act* (see 5.5 below). It was not disputed that a greenhouse was a building and Goff LJ noted that a greenhouse was not just a garden under glass, but that it was a building with apertures, i.e. the glass roof and sides.

Harris v De Pinna (1886)

The plaintiff had a permanent structure on his property, used for storing and seasoning timber and showing it to customers. It was divided into floors with open unglazed ends which allowed for drying of the timber and admitting light. It appeared that the timber was piled up in different ways, from time to time, so that light came in through different apertures. The judge decided that this structure was not a building (see 3.4.2.2 above). On appeal, the Court of Appeal did not deal with the question of whether the structure was a building. Instead, it decided that in order for a right to light to be acquired by prescription, the plaintiff must demonstrate that the light had come into the building by the same, definite mode or means of access. The plaintiff had failed to demonstrate that the structure had continually enjoyed light through a definite access and no right to light had therefore been acquired.

3.4.3 For the 20-year period before commencement of the action

Section 3 provides that, after 20 years' enjoyment, the right to light becomes absolute and indefeasible. This section must be read in conjunction with section 4, which provides that the 20-year period must be the period immediately before an action is brought in relation to the right to light.

This leads to some surprising results:

- If light has been enjoyed for 20, 30 or 40 years, there will be no right to light until an action has been brought.
- If after, say, 40 years' enjoyment and before an action is brought, there is an interruption of more than a year (see 3.4.5 below in relation to interruptions), no right will have been acquired.
- If after, say, 40 years' enjoyment and before an action is brought, the light is enjoyed by consent for a period (see 3.4.6 below), for example, to avoid a dispute, no right will have been acquired.

The 20-year period required to establish a right to light under the doctrine of lost modern grant does not need to be the 20 years before the action, but could be an earlier period of time provided that there has been no abandonment (see 4.4 below in relation to abandonment). There are therefore situations in which a claimant will be able to succeed under the doctrine of lost modern grant, but not under the *Prescription Act*.

Colls v Home and Colonial Stores Ltd (1904)

This is the leading case on the amount of light to which the dominant property is entitled once a right has been acquired by prescription (see Chapter 5). Although not part of the actual decision (or *ratio*) of the case, Lord Macnaghten also explained the law in relation to the 20-year period. He stated that section 3 must be read together with section 4 of the *Prescription Act*. This meant that the access and use of light to a building for a period of 20 years did not create an absolute and indefeasible right immediately at the end of that 20-year period. Instead, an absolute and indefeasible right to light only arose if the 20-year period was the 20 years before an action was brought.

Hyman v Van den Bergh (1908)

A cowshed stood on the plaintiff's land. In 1898, the defendant erected boards on his adjacent land, obstructing the access of light to the cowshed. The following year, the plaintiff's tenant agreed to pay the defendant 1 shilling per annum to keep his windows free from obstruction. The defendant then left the windows unobstructed until 1906, when the tenant left, at which time he reinstated the obstruction. The plaintiff then claimed an injunction, arguing that he had a right to light under section 3 of the *Prescription Act*. No claim was pleaded under the doctrine of lost modern grant.

The Court of Appeal applied Lord Macnaghten's explanation of the 20-year period in *Colls v Home and Colonial Stores Ltd*. It held that sections 3 and 4 of the *Prescription Act* must be read together and that the only period of time for the court to consider was the 20-year period before the action was brought. For over six years of that period, the light had been enjoyed by agreement. The plaintiff had not therefore acquired a right under the *Prescription Act*. It did not matter, for the purpose of a claim under the Act, that the plaintiff might be able to prove enjoyment of light for a 20-year period before the agreement.

Marine & General Mutual Life Assurance Society v St James' Real Estate Co (1991)

The plaintiff claimed damages for interference with its rights to light as a result of a proposed redevelopment of the defendant's adjacent property. The claim was made under the *Prescription Act* and under the doctrine of lost modern grant. The claim under the Act failed because the windows had been blocked in and the light had not been enjoyed for the period of 20 years before the action. The claim for lost modern grant, however, succeeded.

Some of the cases pre-dating *Colls v Home and Colonial Stores Ltd* (1904) need to be treated with care as they were decided on the basis that a right to light was absolutely and indefeasibly acquired under section 3 of the *Prescription Act* after 20 years' enjoyment, even if the action began many years later. As can be seen from the cases summarised above, this is not correct.

3.4.4 The light has actually been enjoyed

Under section 3 of the Act, a claimant must show that his building has actually enjoyed the access of light for the 20-year period.

The cases of *Courtauld v Legh* and *Collis v Laugher* (see 3.4.2.1 above) demonstrate that it is not necessary for the owner to have occupied the premises in respect of which a right to light is claimed or for the premises to be fit for habitation.

There have also been a number of cases in which the court has considered whether the obstruction of windows by the owner/occupier of the dominant property prevents the acquisition of the right. On the one hand, continuous user is not necessary, meaning that a right to light can still be acquired even if shutters are often closed. On the other hand, blocking of the windows may prevent acquisition of the right (even if it would not be sufficient to amount to abandonment: as to which see 4.4 below).

Cooper v Straker (1888)

The plaintiff had a warehouse used for the storage of wool. The windows to the warehouse had steel shutters which were generally kept shut except when the business of the warehouse required them to be opened. This was infrequent, particularly on the lower floors. The defendant argued that the plaintiff had failed to demonstrate sufficient user to entitle him to a right to light.

It was held that 'enjoyed' for the purpose of section 3 of the *Prescription Act* did not mean there had to be continuous use. It meant having the amenity or advantage of using the access to light. The judge considered that, where windows had moveable shutters, which were opened at the owner's pleasure for the admission of light, a right to light would be acquired after 20 years, if he opened them at any time he pleased during that period and provided that there was no interruption of access (as to which see 3.4.5 below).

Smith v Baxter (1900)

The plaintiff and the defendant owned adjoining premises. The defendant intended to increase the height of his building and the plaintiff alleged that this would interfere with his rights to light. One issue was whether rights to light had been acquired under the *Prescription Act* in relation to two windows, which had been boarded up, and a third, which had been covered with open shelving, for more than a year prior to the action being brought. The judge held (relying on *Cooper v Straker*) that continuous user was not necessary in order to acquire a right to light under the *Prescription Act*. The need for continuous user would mean that shops which closed their shutters one day a week would not acquire rights and would be inconsistent with the fact that the right is not lost by demolition and rebuilding (as to which see 4.5.1 below). He stated that non-user which would not be sufficient to amount to abandonment might be enough to prevent the acquisition of a right under the Act. He held that the boarding, which completely excluded the light, prevented a right to light being acquired. However, as the shelving did not entirely exclude the light, but allowed a substantial portion through, a right had been acquired under the *Prescription Act* in relation to the third window.

Marine & General Mutual Life Assurance Society v St James' Real Estate Co (1991)

The plaintiff and defendant companies owned adjoining properties. The defendant proposed reconstructing its property and the plaintiff claimed damages for interference with its right to light. The windows on the first, second and third floor had been blocked in, although apertures were apparently still visible. The plaintiff claimed that it had acquired a right to light under the *Prescription Act* (among other grounds). However, the judge held that the plaintiff was unable to rely on the Act in relation to these windows because, as the windows had been blocked in, the light had not been enjoyed for the 20 years before the commencement of the action. In relation to the claim based on lost modern grant, the defendant unsuccessfully argued that the blocking in of the windows amounted to an abandonment (see 4.4 below).

Tamares (Vincent Square) Ltd v Fairpoint Properties (Vincent Square) Ltd (2007)

The claimant and defendant owned adjoining premises. The defendant had demolished an existing single storey flat roofed building and replaced it with a three storey building with a pitched roof. The claimant alleged that the new building interfered with its right to light to certain windows, including two in the lobby which had been completely blocked up by internal panelling throughout the 20-year period necessary to acquire a right to light under the *Prescription Act*. This panelling was part of the design of the entrance lobby. The defendant argued that the claimant had acquired no right to light through the lobby windows. The judge agreed. Where boarding was used to block the entrance of light, it could not be argued that the light illuminated the rear side of the blockage and therefore allowed a right to be acquired. There was no actual enjoyment for the 20-year period, as required by the *Prescription Act*.

There is also a question as to whether demolition or alteration of the building during the 20-year period will prevent the right being acquired. Demolition and alteration have been considered by the courts in cases relating to extinguishment of rights already acquired (see Chapter 4). These issues have rarely been considered in the context of rights which have not yet been acquired.

Nonetheless, it has been held in one case that the demolition or alteration of a building during the 20-year period over which the right is being acquired will not prevent its acquisition if the new window receives a substantial part of the light received by the old window. However, the courts have not yet considered the effect of the demolition of a building which leaves the site vacant for a number of years. It is suggested that this would have the effect of preventing actual enjoyment of the light for a period of years and that it could therefore prevent the acquisition of a right to light under the Act.

Andrews v Waite (1907)

The plaintiff leased and occupied premises adjoining a property leased by the defendant. During the 20 years before the action, the plaintiff's premises had been substantially altered once and demolished and re-built on another occasion. The defendant then constructed a wall and buildings over 50 ft high on his land very close to the boundary and the plaintiff brought an action against him claiming an injunction preventing the defendant from building in a way which would interfere with his light.

The judge found that a substantial amount of light which came through the new windows had also come through the old ground and first floor windows. Previous cases (such as *Scott v Pape* (1886)) had considered whether a right which had already been acquired could be lost by demolition or alteration (see Chapter 4). He held that the same principles applied both after a right had been acquired and during the period necessary for its acquisition under section 3 of the *Prescription Act*. He therefore held that the alteration and demolition of the plaintiff's premises did not prevent the right from being acquired under the Act.

3.4.5 Without interruption

A claimant will be prevented from acquiring a right to light under section 3 of the *Prescription Act* if he acquiesces in or submits to a servient owner or occupier's interruption of his access to light for a year or more (see section 4 of the *Prescription Act*). Interruptions can be either by physical obstructions (such as a wall or a screen) or notional obstructions under the *Rights of Light Act* 1959.

3.4.5.1 Physical obstructions

Physical interruptions include the construction of a wall or the erection of a screen. However, a fluctuating obstruction, such as the piling up of crates and boxes to different levels at different times, will not be sufficient to constitute an interruption.

Presland v Bingham (1889)

The plaintiffs and the defendant, a stonemason, owned adjoining premises. The defendant substantially raised the height of the party wall and the plaintiffs began an action, claiming that the defendant had interfered with the light to their skylight. The defendant argued that the plaintiffs had not acquired a right to light under the *Prescription Act* because he had interrupted the light for several years by piling empty packing-cases up against the party wall above the height of the wall. The evidence was conflicting as to the height of the packing cases. It was clear, however, that the cases were moved from time to time and that the level fluctuated between high, low and no obstruction at all.

The Court of Appeal held that the interruption did not fall within section 4 of the *Prescription Act*. It was fluctuating, uncertain and intermittent and there was no satisfactory evidence on which it could be held that it had lasted continuously for one year. The plaintiffs had therefore acquired a right to light. It was also held that, if the obstruction was of a permanent character, the burden was on the plaintiff to prove that it did not continue for a year with his acquiescence; but, if the obstruction was of a temporary character, the burden was on the defendant to prove that there had been an obstruction for a year in which the plaintiff acquiesced.

Acts of the claimant himself, such as boarding up a window, do not amount to interruption (although, in appropriate circumstances, they may prevent the light being actually enjoyed (see 3.4.4 above) or amount to abandonment (see Chapter 4)).

Smith v Baxter (1900)

The plaintiff and the defendant owned adjoining premises. The defendant intended to increase the height of his building and the plaintiff alleged that this would interfere with his rights to light. One issue was whether rights to light had been acquired under the *Prescription Act* in relation to two windows, which had been boarded up, and a third, which had been covered with open shelving, for more than a year prior to the action being brought. The defendant argued, amongst other things, that the boarding and shelving constituted an interruption for the purposes of the *Prescription Act.* The judge held, however, that it did not and that the term 'interruption' refers to an adverse obstruction and not a mere discontinuance of user.

Where an interruption occurs, it is always sensible to start proceedings within a year. However, where an interruption has occurred for a year or more, it will not prevent the acquisition of a right to light unless it has been acquiesced in or submitted to by the claimant. The burden is on the claimant to prove that he has not submitted to or acquiesced in the interruption. The courts have held that protests to the person creating the obstruction can demonstrate non-submission or non-acquiescence. Complaints to friends and family will not be enough. The longer the period between the last complaint to the defendant and the commencement of proceedings, the harder it is likely to be for the claimant to prove that he did not submit to or acquiesce in the interruption.

Glover v Coleman (1874)

The plaintiff had enjoyed the access of light through his workshop window over the defendant's land for more than 20 years. The defendant then constructed a building which obstructed the light some 14 months before an action was commenced by the plaintiff. Although the plaintiff had not started proceedings earlier or tried to remove the obstruction, he did complain on more than one occasion to the defendant. The judge directed that a verdict be entered for the plaintiff. The defendant appealed.

The Court of Appeal considered the meaning of acquiescence and submission for the purpose of section 4 of the *Prescription Act*. It held that:

- Acquiescence did not mean an active agreement but what might be called a tacit or silent agreement by someone who is satisfied to submit.
- Submission meant submission without being satisfied to submit and without any direct act of opposition, although discontent may be made apparent by some expression or act.

The Court of Appeal also held that whether there was submission or acquiescence was a question of fact and of degree. Mere grumbling or complaining to friends or family would not be sufficient evidence of non-submission or non-acquiescence. It found that, given the complaints made to the defendant and the fact that little more than a year had passed, there was evidence that the plaintiff had not acquiesced in or submitted to the interruption. The defendant's appeal therefore failed.

Davies v Du Paver (1953)

This case concerned rights of pasturage rather than rights to light. The Court of Appeal dealt with the issue of interruption under the *Prescription Act*.

The defendant put up a fence which interfered with the plaintiff's use of the land in question. While the fence was being erected, the plaintiff protested vigorously and his solicitors wrote stating that legal proceedings would be taken if the interference continued. After the fence was completed, the plaintiff made no further protest until more than a year later, when the plaintiff began proceedings, claiming rights under the *Prescription Act*. The judge held that the plaintiff had proved that he and his predecessors had exercised rights of pasturage for over 60 years. It was clear from the facts that there had been an interruption for more than one year, but the judge held that the plaintiff had not submitted to or acquiesced in the interruption for one year. The defendant appealed.

The Court of Appeal held that it was a question of fact whether there had been a submission or acquiescence and that the judge's finding of fact that there had not been submission or acquiescence should not be reversed. Birkett LJ, however, stated that it was not easy to reach a conclusion on the facts of the case. It was necessary to consider both the fact that nothing overt was done for over a year and the fact that there had previously been strong protests. Morris LJ stated that, as time went by, it might well be that silence and inaction could be interpreted as submission or acquiescence, but the date at which this occurred was a question of fact for the judge.

Dance v Triplow (1991)

The plaintiff and the defendant owned adjoining houses. In November 1980, the defendant completed the construction of a two storey extension to his house. The plaintiff began proceedings in August 1984 complaining that the extension infringed his right to light to the window to the spare bedroom. He claimed that he had acquired a right to light under the *Prescription Act*. There was some evidence that the plaintiff had complained to the defendant about the loss of light in or before February 1982. It was common ground that no complaint was made by the plaintiff or his solicitor between that date and the date the action was commenced, although the plaintiff's solicitor did write to the defendant about another matter. The defendant argued that the plaintiff had submitted to or acquiesced in the interruption.

The Court of Appeal held (referring to *Presland v Bingham* (1889)) that the burden was on the plaintiff to prove that, at the time he commenced the action, the interruption had lasted for less than one year or that, if it had lasted for more than a year, that he did not submit to or acquiesce in it. In order to demonstrate non-submission or non-acquiescence, it was necessary for a plaintiff not only to feel discontented, but also to communicate his discontent to the defendant. The Court of Appeal accepted that if there had been evidence of strong complaint by the plaintiff periodically up to and shortly before February 1982, it should have been clear to the defendants for some time afterwards that the plaintiff was not submitting or acquiescing. However, it held on the facts of the case that the failure to communicate with the defendants for two and half years could only be construed as amounting to submission to or acquiescence in the interruption.

3.4.5.2 Notional obstructions – *Rights of Light Act* 1959

The *Rights of Light Act* 1959 was introduced to make it easier for a neighbour to interrupt a dominant owner's enjoyment of the access of light over his property and therefore to prevent the acquisition of a right to light under the *Prescription Act.* Before the Act, the only way of doing this was by physically constructing a building or erecting a screen or hoardings. Issues such as expense and the need for planning permission made this difficult. The *Rights of Light Act* 1959 allows registration of a notional, rather than an actual obstruction. The Act treats the notional structure as if it were an opaque structure on the servient land. The Act is supplemented by Rules 21–24 of the *Lands Tribunal Rules* 1996.

The procedure for registering a notice involves the following steps:

- Application to the Lands Tribunal for a certificate, certifying that adequate notice has been given to the persons likely to be affected.
- Application to the local authority to register a notice. The application must identify the dominant and servient land and state the position and dimensions of the notional structure.
- Registration by the local authority of the notice as a local land charge. Unless cancelled, it has effect for the period of one year beginning with the date of registration of the notice.

In appropriate cases, the Lands Tribunal may issue a temporary certificate, certifying that that the case is one of exceptional urgency and that a notice should be registered immediately as a temporary notice. A temporary notice cannot last more than six months. Once notice has been given to the person(s) likely to be affected, the Lands Tribunal issues a definitive certificate.

Section 3(6) of the *Rights of Light Act* 1959 provides that, for the purposes of interruption under section 4 of the *Prescription Act*, everyone with an interest in the dominant building is deemed to acquiesce in the obstruction until an action is brought in respect of the obstruction. Therefore, in order to avoid submitting to or acquiescing in the obstruction for a year, the owner of the dominant property needs to bring proceedings within one year of the registration of the notice. Where a temporary notice has been registered, followed by a definitive notice, the period of one year will begin on the date of registration of the temporary notice.

Bowring Services Ltd v Scottish Widows' Fund & Life Assurance Society (1995)

The plaintiff had a long leasehold interest in a building which received light over an adjoining site owned by the defendant. The defendant started to construct buildings on its site in a way that the plaintiff claimed would interfere with its light. The plaintiff brought proceedings against the defendant claiming that its property had acquired a right to light by common law prescription, lost modern grant and under the *Prescription Act*. The defendant registered a temporary obstruction notice under the *Rights of Light Act* 1959 more than one year before the plaintiff started the action. The definitive certificate was issued less than one year before the action began. The defendant applied to strike out the plaintiff's claim as an abuse of process.

The judge allowed the defendant's application and struck out the plaintiff's claim. He struck out the claims for common law prescription and lost modern grant (see 3.2.1 and 3.3.2.1 above). In relation to the claim under the *Prescription Act*, the judge held that the one year period under the *Rights of Light Act* 1959 began on the date of registration of the temporary notice, not the definitive notice. The defendant had therefore obstructed/interrupted the plaintiff's light for more than one year by the time that the plaintiff commenced proceedings and the plaintiff therefore had not acquired a right to light under the *Prescription Act*.

If proceedings are begun within one year of registration of the notice, section 3(5) of the *Rights of Light Act* 1959 provides that the remedies available to the claimant are a declaration and an order directing the registration of the notice to be cancelled or varied.

Hawker v Tomalin (1969)

The plaintiff owned property next to the defendant's site, which was vacant as a result of bomb damage in 1942. The defendant registered a notice under the *Rights of Light Act* 1959 identifying a notional obstruction to the plaintiff's light. The defendant claimed that the bombed buildings had been the same height as those in the notice. Within a year, the plaintiff began proceedings for a declaration that the defendant was not entitled to obstruct the access of light, alternatively asking for the notice to be varied. The judge decided that the notional obstruction infringed the plaintiff's right to light and ordered the cancellation of the notice. On appeal to the Court of Appeal, after detailed consideration of the location of the bomb damaged buildings, the court made a declaration that the height of the original notional obstruction would infringe the plaintiff's right to light and made an order varying the notice so as to specify obstruction of a height which did not infringe the plaintiff's right to light.

3.4.5.3 Nineteen years and one day's enjoyment

The *Prescription Act* requires 20 years' enjoyment before a right is acquired. However, the effect of the provisions of the Act relating to interruption is that if there has been enjoyment for 19 years and one day followed by an obstruction, the claimant will acquire an absolute and indefeasible right under section 3. In this situation, the claimant cannot bring an action until the 20 years have expired.

Lord Battersea v Commissioners of Sewers for the City of London (1895)

The plaintiffs were lessees of land opposite land belonging to the defendant. In October 1875 buildings had been demolished on the defendant's land and, since then, only low level buildings had been built. However, in 1895 the defendant started to construct higher office buildings. The plaintiffs started an action in July 1895 claiming an injunction to restrain the defendant from interfering with their rights to light under section 3 of the *Prescription Act*. This was only 19 and three-quarter years after the demolition of the original buildings. The judge held that no action could be brought until the expiry of the full 20-year period.

3.4.6 Without written consent or agreement

A right to light cannot be acquired under the *Prescription Act* where it has been enjoyed, for any part of the prescriptive period, by written consent or agreement which was expressly made for the purpose of preventing the dominant owner or occupier from acquiring a right to light.

In a simple case, the agreement could be in the form of a letter acknowledging that the light is enjoyed by permission or in return for payment. Such a letter written by the tenant in occupation of the property in relation to which a right to light is subsequently claimed will bind him and the freehold owner.

Easton v Isted (1903)

In this case, the plaintiff argued that he had acquired a right to light under the *Prescription Act* in respect of a skylight or glazed roof, which had originally been part of a conservatory. The main issue was whether a written agreement by the plaintiff to pay the defendant one shilling per year to allow the windows in the conservatory to open on to and overlook the defendant's property covered the skylight or glazed roof. The judge held the plaintiff's window or skylight would fall within section 3 of the *Prescription Act* unless the light was enjoyed by consent or agreement in writing (see 3.4.2.3 above). However, he held that the word 'windows' in the agreement included skylights and, therefore, that no right had been acquired under the Act because the light had been enjoyed by agreement. The Court of Appeal upheld the judge's decision.

Hyman v Van den Bergh (1908)

A cowshed stood on the plaintiff's land. In 1898, the defendant erected boards on his adjacent land, obstructing the access of light to the cowshed. The following year, the plaintiff's tenant agreed to pay the defendant one shilling per year to keep his windows free from obstruction. The defendant then left the windows unobstructed until 1906, when the tenant left, at which time he reinstated the obstruction. The plaintiff then claimed an injunction preventing such an obstruction, arguing that he had a right to light under section 3 of the *Prescription Act*.

The Court of Appeal dismissed the plaintiff's claim. For over six years of the 20-year period before the action had begun, the light had been enjoyed by agreement. The plaintiff had not therefore acquired a right under the *Prescription Act*, since the agreement by his tenant (who was the person actually enjoying the light) was sufficient to constitute written agreement under section 3 of the Act.

Where the owner of two or more properties sells one of them, an agreement or consent to the enjoyment of light can be contained in the conveyance or lease and therefore prevent the acquisition of a right to light. The courts have considered two types of provision:

- provisions which state that nothing in the conveyance or lease operates expressly or impliedly to grant any easement which is not expressly granted; and
- provisions which reserve to the landlord/vendor the right to build freely on his own retained land as he thinks fit.

The effect of such clauses will depend on their particular wording and the surrounding circumstances. However, generally, the first type of provision simply prevents a right to light being acquired by virtue of the lease or conveyance at the outset: it does not prevent a right subsequently being acquired by prescription. The second type of provision, however, is likely to amount to an agreement or consent to the enjoyment of light for the purposes of section 3 of the *Prescription Act*.

Mitchell v Cantrill (1887)

The owner of two adjoining properties granted a lease of one to the plaintiff. The lease granted all rights, etc. 'except rights, if any, restricting the free use of any adjoining land, or the conversion or appropriation at any time hereafter of such land for building or other purposes, obstructive or otherwise'. More than 20 years later, the defendant who was now a lessee of adjoining land from the same owner, started to build on his land in a way that the plaintiff claimed would affect the rights to light which he claimed to have acquired under the *Prescription Act*. The plaintiff therefore brought proceedings against the defendant claiming an injunction.

The Court of Appeal held that the plaintiff had acquired a right to light under the *Prescription Act*. It held that the exception in the lease did not prevent the plaintiff from acquiring a right to light under the *Prescription Act* where he had enjoyed 20 years' uninterrupted light over the defendant's property. The exception simply prevented the grant of a right to light by way of the lease itself.

Haynes v King (1893)

The plaintiffs leased houses from the Ecclesiastical Commissioners. At the date that the parties entered into the leases, the Commissioners also owned four old houses which were on the opposite side of the street from the plaintiffs' houses. The plaintiffs' leases contained a declaration giving the lessors the 'power, without obtaining any consent from ... the lessee, to deal as they may think fit with any of the premises adjoining or contiguous to the hereditaments hereby demised, and to erect, or suffer to be erected, on such adjoining or contiguous premises, any buildings whatsoever, whether such buildings shall or shall not affect or diminish the light or air which may now, or at any time during the term hereby granted, be enjoyed by the lessee, or the tenants or occupiers of the hereditaments hereby demised'. The plaintiffs enjoyed the access of light to their properties for 20 years without any alterations being made to the Commissioners' four old houses. Thereafter, the Commissioners entered into an agreement with the defendant, under which they agreed to grant the defendant a lease of the four old houses if he demolished and reconstructed them in accordance with approved plans. The plaintiffs brought proceedings against the defendant for interference with rights to light acquired under the *Prescription Act*.

The judge held that the plaintiffs had not acquired rights to light under the *Prescription Act* because their leases prevented them from doing so. He stated that the leases would have given the plaintiffs the right to enjoy light over the defendant's premises, if it had not been for the power in the clause set out above. This clause expressly provided that the enjoyment of light by the lessee was only to exist until the lessors wished to exercise their rights contained in that clause. The clause therefore fell within the exception in section 3 of the *Prescription Act* and prevented the plaintiffs from acquiring a right to light by prescription.

Ruscoe v Grounsell (1903)

John Musgrave sold two cottages to the plaintiff's predecessor (John Atkin). At the same time, a stone tablet was built into the wall of one of the cottages with the following inscription: 'This stone is placed by John Atkin to perpetuate John Musgrave's right to build within nine inches of this and any other building'. Some 85 years later, the plaintiff owned the two cottages and the defendant owned adjoining land. The plaintiff commenced an action against the defendant for obstructing his right to light by building a large shed on his land. The Court of Appeal held that the inscription could not be construed as a consent or agreement 'expressly made for that purpose' within the meaning of section 3 of the *Prescription Act*. Therefore, the plaintiff had acquired a right to light by prescription.

Willoughby v Eckstein (1937)

The plaintiff and defendant were granted leases of adjoining premises by the same landlord. The plaintiff's lease expressly excluded the grant of rights to light or other easements over the premises. It also said that it was subject to 'the adjacent buildings or any of them being at any time or times rebuilt or altered according to plans as to height elevation extent and otherwise ... approved of by the ground landlord'. The plaintiff's building then enjoyed the access of light over the defendant's property for well over 20 years. Thereafter, the defendant pulled down and started to rebuild his premises in a way which the plaintiff claimed would interfere with her rights to light acquired under the *Prescription Act*. The plaintiff therefore brought proceedings against the defendant seeking an injunction.

The judge held that the plaintiff had enjoyed the access of light to her building by written agreement and therefore had not acquired a right to light under section 3 of the *Prescription Act*. The judge held that the exception in the lease for rights to light, together with the right expressly reserved for the adjacent buildings to be rebuilt, was a grant by the plaintiff to the landlord of the right to build during the term of the lease, notwithstanding the effect on the light to the plaintiff's property. It therefore constituted an agreement by the plaintiff that any enjoyment of light to her premises during her lease was by written agreement only.

Marlborough (West End) Ltd v Wilks Head and Eve (1996)

The judge held that whether or not a document constitutes a consent or agreement for the purpose of section 3 of the *Prescription Act* is a question of construction. He said that care must be taken to distinguish between:

- provisions designed to protect the servient owner by negativing the implication of a grant of a right to light; and
- provisions designed to authorise the servient owner at a future date to carry out works or build as he pleases unrestricted by any easement of light and notwithstanding any injury to the light of the dominant property.

The first type of provision does not constitute either a consent or an agreement within section 3 and therefore does not prevent acquisition of light by prescription thereafter. The second type may be construed as a consent or agreement permitting the enjoyment of light before any such building is carried out and accordingly, as a result of the exception in section 3, may prevent the acquisition of a right to light under the Act.

RHJ Ltd v FT Patten (Holdings) Ltd (2008)

The City Council owned a number of pieces of land in Liverpool. In 1980 it granted a lease of one property (the land on which Regian House stood) and retained other land. In 2001, it sold Regian House to the claimant. It had previously sold other land to the defendant. The 1980 lease (a) excepted and reserved out of the lease of Regian House to the Council, its lessees and others the full and free right to construct buildings or rebuild on the land adjoining or opposite to Regian House and (b) provided that nothing contained in the lease was to operate so as to create a grant by way of implication unless an express provision was made in the lease. The lease made no express reference to light. The issue, heard as a preliminary issue, was whether the claimant had acquired a right to light under the *Prescription Act* or whether the terms of the lease set out above constituted an agreement in writing under section 3 and therefore prevented the acquisition of the right.

The Court of Appeal considered the previous case law (in particular, *Marlborough (West End) Ltd v Wilks Head and Eve* (1996), *Mitchell v Cantrill* (1887) and *Willoughby v Eckstein* (1937)) and held that the terms of the lease amounted to an agreement in writing for the purposes of section 3. Therefore no right to light had been acquired by the claimant under the *Prescription Act*. It held that whether a document fell within the exception within section 3 depended on the true construction of the document, in the relevant surrounding circumstances. The clause at (b) above prevented the immediate acquisition of a right to light by virtue of the lease. As to the clause at (a):

- there was no need for the agreement to refer expressly to light in order for it to amount to an agreement in writing for the purpose of section 3;
- the phrase 'expressly made or given for that purpose' in section 3 could be satisfied by an express provision in the document which, on its true construction, has the effect of rendering the enjoyment of light permissive, consensual or capable of being terminated or interfered with by the adjoining owner and which was therefore inconsistent with the enjoyment becoming absolute and indefeasible after 20 years;
- it was clear that the parties were well aware of the importance of rights to light; that the acquisition of rights to light in favour of the leased property was clearly a possibility; and that rights to light would be one of the more significant constraints on the landlord's ability to build as it thought fit. In the light of all these factors, the

proper construction of the clause at (a) above was that it was intended to affect the light to Regian House, even though light was not mentioned in the clause.

The clause at (a) therefore amounted to an agreement in writing for the purposes of section 3 of the Act and prevented the acquisition of a right to light under the Act.

3.4.7 By and against whom can a right to light be acquired?

Unlike rights to light acquired by other methods of prescription, rights to light acquired under the Act can be acquired by and against leaseholders, as well as freeholders. Where the freehold of two properties is owned by the same landlord, a right to light can be acquired by the lessee of one property against the lessee of the other and the common landlord. The right will also be enforceable against the future owners of the servient property.

Morgan v Fear (1907)

Numbers 16 and 18 were owned by the same freehold owner, the Corporation of Aberystwyth. The plaintiff (Fear) was a lessee of no. 16 and the defendant (Morgan) was the lessee of no. 18. The defendant raised the height of a wall on his premises and interfered with the plaintiff's light. The plaintiff began an action. The House of Lords (confirming a doctrine set out in the earlier cases of *Frewen v Philips* (1861) and *Mitchell v Cantrill* (1887)) held that a lessee who had enjoyed access of light for 20 years without interruption over an adjoining property acquired an absolute and indefeasible right to light against the other property and that this right existed against the adjoining lessee and the common landlord, as well as against all future owners of the adjoining property.

However, under the *Prescription Act*, rights to light cannot be acquired against the Crown.

Perry v Eames (1891)

The plaintiffs claimed a right to light to their houses over the site of the old Bankruptcy Court in the City of London. At the time of the action, the site was owned by the defendant. However, until some five years earlier, the property had been owned by the Crown. The judge held that no right to light had been acquired under the *Prescription Act* because the site had been owned by the Crown until five years earlier. His reasoning was that section 2 of the *Prescription Act* specifically referred to the Crown, but that section 2, which applied to rights of way and other easements, did not apply to rights to light. Section 3 of the *Prescription Act* applied to rights to light, but did not specifically mention the Crown. The judge therefore concluded, on the basis of the general rule that the Crown is not bound by a statute, unless named in it, that section 3 did not apply to the Crown. The plaintiff's claim under the *Prescription Act* therefore failed.

Wheaton v Maple & Co (1893)

The plaintiff built two houses on his land in 1852. The defendants, who leased the adjacent land from the Crown, then constructed new buildings on that land and obstructed the light to the plaintiff's houses. The plaintiff claimed that he had acquired rights to light under the *Prescription Act* (among other bases). The Court of Appeal held (referring to *Perry v Eames* (1891)) that section 3 of the *Prescription Act* did not apply to the Crown and that section 2, which did apply to the Crown, did not apply to rights to light. It also held that the plaintiff could not acquire rights against the defendant lessees under the *Prescription Act* for the remainder of the defendants' lease since the Act could not create a limited right to light against a lessee in circumstances in which the landlord could not be bound. The position was different from that in *Morgan v Fear* (1907) (see above) because in this case the landlord, the Crown, could not be bound.

3.4.8 No need to show enjoyment 'as of right'

Unlike prescriptive rights to light acquired at common law and under the doctrine of lost modern grant (see 3.2 and 3.3 above), a claimant claiming that he is entitled to a right to light under section 3 does not have to show that he has enjoyed the light that he has received 'as of right'.

Colls v Home and Colonial Stores Ltd (1904)

This is the leading case on the amount of light to which the dominant property is entitled once a right has been acquired by prescription (see Chapter 5 below). Lord Lindley also explained that there was no requirement under section 3 of the *Prescription Act* to prove enjoyment 'as of right'. All that needed to be proved was 20 years' use and enjoyment, without interruption and without consent.

3.5 SUMMARY OF CRITERIA APPLICABLE TO THE THREE METHODS OF PRESCRIPTION

As set out above, different criteria apply to each of the three methods of prescription. A summary of the key similarities and differences is set out in the following table:

Method of acquisition	Period of use required	Must use be 'as of right'?	By and against freeholders only?	Against the Crown?
Common law	Since time immemorial (1189)	Yes	Yes	Yes
Lost modern grant	20 years at any time	Yes	Yes	Yes
Prescription Act	20 years immediately before action	No	No	No

4
Extinguishment

4.1 INTRODUCTION

A right to light can be extinguished by:

- agreement;
- unity of ownership;
- abandonment;
- demolition or alteration of the dominant property; or
- statute.

Some of the cases on extinguishment (e.g. *Tapling v Jones* (1865) and *Scott v Pape* (1886)) which pre-date *Colls v Home and Colonial Stores Ltd* (1904) need to be treated with care as the courts often assumed that the 20-year period necessary to acquire a right to light under the *Prescription Act* did not need to be the 20 years immediately before proceedings were brought. As explained in Chapter 3 (at 3.4.3), this assumption was not correct. The principles relating to extinguishment in these cases remain good law and applicable to cases where rights to light have been acquired by common law prescription or lost modern grant. However, in *Prescription Act* cases nowadays, the need to establish enjoyment for the 20-year period immediately before the action will mean that the question for the court to determine is likely to be whether a right has been acquired and not whether it has been extinguished.

4.2 EXTINGUISHMENT BY AGREEMENT

The owners of the dominant and servient properties may agree to release a right to light. This is often called an express release.

As a right to light is an interest in land, its release must be in writing in order to satisfy the requirements of section 53 of LPA

1925. The conveyance of a legal interest (as opposed to an equitable interest) must be by deed in accordance with section 52 of LPA 1925. The legal requirements for a deed are set out in section 2 of the *Law of Property (Miscellaneous Provisions) Act* 1989.

4.3 EXTINGUISHMENT BY UNITY OF OWNERSHIP

Where two properties are in separate freehold ownership, are not leased and a right to light is acquired over one property by the owner of the other, the subsequent unity of the freehold ownership of the two properties will extinguish the right to light. This is because it is not possible to have an easement (including a right to light) over one's own property.

However, where a right to light has been acquired under the *Prescription Act* by or against a leasehold owner (see 3.4.7 above), the subsequent unity of the freehold ownership of the properties will not extinguish this right. As explained at 4.1 above, however, this situation will rarely arise nowadays as the issue in court proceedings in relation to a right claimed under the *Prescription Act* will usually be whether the right has been acquired and not whether it has been extinguished.

Richardson v Graham (1908)

The Court of Appeal held that unity of the freehold ownership of two properties did not extinguish a right to light, where the leasehold of the dominant property was in separate ownership.

4.4 EXTINGUISHMENT BY ABANDONMENT

It is possible for an owner to abandon a right to light, whether it has been acquired by grant, by reservation or by prescription. In such a case, the right becomes extinguished. In order for there to be an effective abandonment, it is necessary to demonstrate a clear intention by the dominant owner to abandon the right.

The courts have sometimes also taken into account whether the actions of the dominant owner (for example, in building a blank wall where there were previously windows) have been relied on by the servient owner, so that it would be unjust to allow the dominant owner then to reassert his right to light. This appears to be a type of estoppel: i.e. a situation where A alters his position in reliance on the actions of B and the court decides that it would not be fair for B, afterwards, to reassert his legal rights.

Abandonment can be extremely difficult to demonstrate. The older cases show that a long period of time over which windows have been blocked up may, but will not always, be enough to show an intention to abandon the right to light. More recent cases (see, e.g. *Tehidy Minerals Ltd v Norman* (1971), which was not a rights to light case) have identified that the test for the abandonment of an easement is whether the person entitled to the easement has demonstrated a fixed intention never at any time thereafter to assert the right himself or to attempt to transmit it to anyone else.

Lawrence v Obee (1814)

This was a claim for nuisance as a result of smells from the defendant's toilet, rather than a claim for a right to light. However, it is relevant as it related to the effect of blocking up a window. There had been a window in the wall of the plaintiff's house, adjacent to the defendant's property, but this had been bricked up for more than 20 years. The defendant then built a toilet. The plaintiff subsequently created a window in the position of the previous window and complained of a nuisance (namely, the smells from the toilet). The claim was dismissed. It was held that, as the window had been shut up for 20 years, it was as if it had never existed. The judge considered that the plaintiff had brought the nuisance upon herself by re-creating the window.

Moore v Rawson (1824)

The plaintiff and defendant owned adjoining premises. Some 17 years before the action, the plaintiff's premises had included a weaver's shop with windows overlooking the defendant's land. The shop was pulled down and replaced with a stable which, instead of windows, had a blank wall adjacent to the defendant's premises. About three years before the action, the defendant constructed a building next to the blank stable wall. Thereafter, the plaintiff formed a window in the stable wall in the same place as one of the original windows and claimed that the defendant's building interfered with his right to light through the new window.

The court held that the right to light had been abandoned. Abbott CJ stated that a person who pulled down his house, erected a blank wall in its place and allowed the blank wall to remain for a considerable period of time, would need to show that this apparent abandonment was intended only to be temporary rather than perpetual and that he intended to resume the enjoyment of the right within a reasonable period of time. The plaintiff could not show this. In addition, Abbott CJ considered that by building a blank wall, the dominant owner could have induced another person to buy the adjoining land for building purposes and that it would be unjust if he were then able to prevent that person from building.

Stokoe v Singers (1857)

The plaintiffs' predecessors had blocked up windows by putting rubble and plaster over the inside of them, some 20 years before the action. On the outside, iron bars (which had secured the windows) remained in place. Thereafter, the defendant purchased adjoining land and proposed to build on it in a manner which would have interfered with the access of light through the blocked windows. The plaintiffs then asserted their rights to light by reopening the blocked windows. There was a dispute as to whether the windows had been blocked for a temporary purpose or whether this had been done with the intention of permanently altering the condition of the building.

The case was tried by jury. The trial judge directed the jury to find for the plaintiffs unless they believed that the plaintiffs' predecessors had blocked the windows with the intention of abandoning them forever or that the windows had been kept closed so as to lead the defendant to alter his position in the reasonable belief that the rights to light had been permanently abandoned. The jury decided, in favour of the plaintiffs, that the rights to light had not been abandoned. The defendant's application for a retrial on the grounds that the judge had misdirected the jury failed. The appeal court held that the judge's direction to the jury was correct in law.

Tehidy Minerals Ltd v Norman (1971)

This case did not concern rights to light, but the Court of Appeal set out a useful test for abandonment. The defendants, who owned farms, claimed rights to graze animals on a down owned by the plaintiff. The down was requisitioned by the Ministry of Agriculture and Fisheries in 1941. In 1954, licences were issued to the commoners' association, of which the defendants were members, to use the down for grazing. In 1960, further arrangements were made between the plaintiff and the association in relation to grazing on the down. It was held that the defendants had acquired prescriptive rights to graze on the down by 1941. It was argued by the plaintiff, however, that arrangements in 1960 in relation to grazing, which meant that the defendants did not use their common rights to graze, but instead that the association had control of grazing on the down, amounted to abandonment of the defendants' rights. The Court of Appeal decided that there was no abandonment because the 1960 agreement was of a temporary and terminable nature. It was held that abandonment of an easement could only be treated as having taken place where the person entitled to it had demonstrated a fixed intention never at any time thereafter to assert the right himself or to attempt to transmit it to anyone else.

Marine & General Mutual Life Assurance Society v St James' Real Estate Co Ltd (1991)

The plaintiff and defendant companies owned adjoining properties. At the rear of the plaintiff's property was an open space between it and the defendant's property which provided a light well. The defendant proposed to reconstruct its property, which would have removed the light well, and to increase the height of the wall and roof of the defendant's property. The plaintiff claimed damages for interference with its rights to light. The windows on the first, second and third floor had been blocked in (although apparently the apertures were still visible). The defendant argued that the plaintiff had abandoned its right to light. However, the judge decided, applying the test for abandonment in *Tehidy Minerals Ltd v Norman*, that the right acquired by lost modern grant had not been abandoned. In relation to the claim under the *Prescription Act*, the question of abandonment did not arise because the right had not been acquired, as light had not been enjoyed for 20 years before commencement of the action (see 3.4.4 above).

In the context of rights of way, the Court of Appeal has recently made it clear that abandonment is not lightly to be inferred and that the dominant owner must manifest an intention to abandon the right.

CDC2020 plc v George Ferreira (2005)

The claimant claimed a right of way, which had not been used for 30 years, over the defendant's land. However, the Court of Appeal agreed with the trial judge that there had been no abandonment. It held that, in order for there to be abandonment, the dominant owner must manifest an intention to abandon the right, and in order to do so, must make it clear that his intention is that neither he nor his successors in title should thereafter make any use of the right. Abandonment was not to be lightly inferred. In this case, although substantial works had been carried out to the land, they did not justify an inference that the then owner intended to abandon the right of way forever so that neither he nor his successors could ever resume its exercise.

Williams and Hibbit v Sandy Lane (Chester) Ltd (2006)

The claimants claimed declarations that they were entitled to rights of way (via a primary and a secondary route) over the defendant's land. The question of abandonment arose in relation to the secondary route, which had not been used for nearly 30 years because the claimants found the primary route more convenient. They had fenced their land so as to obstruct the secondary route and had carried out earthworks which made walking along the path difficult, but not impossible. The Court of Appeal held that they had not abandoned the right of way. It was not lost by non-user alone, even over many years; what was required was an intention on the part of the dominant owner to abandon the right. The

Court decided that there was nothing in the evidence to support an intention to abandon the right to use the secondary route.

As illustrated by the cases referred to above, blocking up windows is not necessarily sufficient to amount to abandonment. However, blocking up windows can prevent a right to light being acquired under the *Prescription Act* (see 3.4.4 above).

Smith v Baxter (1900)

This case concerned whether the blocking of windows prevented the acquisition of rights to light under the *Prescription Act* (see 3.4.4 above). The judge observed that non-user, which would not be sufficient to establish an abandonment of a right already acquired, may be enough to prevent the acquisition of a right under the *Prescription Act*.

4.5 EXTINGUISHMENT BY DEMOLITION OR ALTERATION OF DOMINANT PROPERTY

Over the years, defendants have argued that the acts of demolishing a building, substantially altering it or changing the shape, size, precise location or plane of the windows will extinguish a right to light. There is an overlap between the cases dealing with this issue and those dealing with abandonment (see 4.4 above). Demolition and alteration do not, of themselves, cause the right to be lost, although demolition may suspend the right temporarily. The important question in relation to new and altered buildings is whether the claimant can demonstrate to the court's satisfaction that there is sufficient coincidence between the new and the old windows. If he can, the right to light will not generally be lost.

4.5.1 Demolition

The mere act of demolition of a building will not extinguish rights to light. This is clearly the case where the dominant owner intends to rebuild with the windows in the same places. Even where there is no clear evidence of rebuilding proposals, whilst the enjoyment of the right may be suspended, it will continue to exist until it is abandoned. Abandonment is dealt with at 4.4 above.

Staight v Burn (1869)

The plaintiffs and defendants owned adjoining premises. The plaintiffs, who had acquired rights to light through windows in the west wall of their property, demolished the building to enlarge it, but left the west wall standing to preserve the windows. The defendants then started to build a blank wall within 3 ft of the plaintiffs' west wall, blocking light to the windows. The plaintiffs applied for an injunction preventing the continued building of the wall and compelling the defendants to pull down what had already been built. The defendants argued that any injury to the plaintiffs' property would be caused, not by their works, but by the alterations which the plaintiffs planned to the rest of their premises. The Court of Appeal rejected the defendants' argument and concluded that, as the evidence demonstrated that the plaintiffs intended to retain or restore the windows through which they had enjoyed light, nothing that they had done to the property prevented them from enforcing their right to light through those windows. The court ordered an injunction against the defendants, on the basis that the plaintiffs undertook either to retain or restore the original windows.

Ecclesiastical Commissioners v Kino (1880)

The plaintiffs pulled down an ancient church with the intention of selling the site. There were therefore no specific proposals for rebuilding on the site. Whilst the site was vacant, the defendant commenced the erection of buildings which, if completed, would have materially obstructed the access of light to windows occupying the same position as those within the former church building. The plaintiffs therefore commenced an action to restrain the defendant from constructing the buildings to such a height as to interfere with the church's right to light. The defendant argued that the demolition of the church by the plaintiffs extinguished their right to light. The Court of Appeal granted the plaintiffs an interim injunction. It held that the right to light had not been abandoned or brought to an end by the demolition. It still existed, although its enjoyment was suspended after demolition.

4.5.2 Alterations in the building and/or the windows

Where alterations are carried out to the dominant building, the right to light is not usually extinguished provided that there is sufficient coincidence between the existing and the new windows. However, where the alterations to the dominant property block out the majority of the existing light and the adjoining owner's act would not have been an actionable interference previously, the right to light will be extinguished.

Tapling v Jones (1865)

The plaintiff (Mr Jones) carried out a number of alterations to his property, which originally consisted of three storeys with one window on each storey. He lowered the windows in the two lower storeys, but the altered windows both occupied part of the old apertures. The window in the third storey remained unaltered. Two additional storeys were built, each with a new window. Thereafter, the defendant built a new wall which obstructed light to all apertures in the plaintiff's building including the unaltered window on the third storey. The defendant argued that he was entitled to obstruct the new windows, which it was impossible to do without also obstructing the old windows, and that the plaintiff had lost his right to light by altering the old windows.

The House of Lords held that the defendant was not entitled to obstruct the rights to light acquired by prescription in relation to the unaltered window and those parts of the new windows occupying parts of the old apertures. Contrary to the defendant's argument, changing or enlarging the windows did not itself destroy the owner's original right.

Scott v Pape (1886)

The plaintiff, who had acquired rights to light over the defendant's land, pulled down his building and constructed a larger building which was completely different in character. Substantial portions of six of the new windows corresponded with three of the old windows in the east wall. This wall had also been brought closer to the defendant's land by between 2 ft 3 in. and 13 in. This also meant that the plane of the new windows was slightly different from that of the old windows. Some years later, the defendant pulled down his buildings and began to build new houses. The plaintiff claimed that the new houses obstructed his rights to light and claimed an injunction restraining the defendant from building so as to interfere with his rights. The judge granted an injunction. The defendant appealed arguing that the plaintiff had lost his rights to light by rebuilding his property and by doing so closer to the defendant's land.

The Court of Appeal held that the six windows occupied a substantial portion of the space formerly occupied by the three windows in the old building and that, by constructing the new building, the plaintiff had not abandoned or lost his rights to light. Nor did the fact that the wall had been moved forward destroy the right: it still received the same light. The plaintiff was therefore entitled to the injunction. The court reviewed the law relating to alterations in buildings and windows and a number of useful propositions can be derived from the judgment:

- It is not the structural identity of the building or of the aperture (i.e. the type of window) which is important, but the position and size of the aperture.
- A right may be lost by such an alteration to the building that the proper inference from the alteration and the conduct of the plaintiff is that it has been abandoned. However, mere alteration or rebuilding of a building will not be enough to demonstrate abandonment.
- Where a window is reduced in size, the plaintiff retains the right to the portion of light coming through the diminished window.
- Where a window is enlarged, the plaintiff still has the right to that portion of light which the old window enjoyed.
- The mere fact of moving back or forward the plane of the wall will not destroy the right. It may do so, if it is substantially moved, so that the light which went through the old window no longer goes through the new window. It will depend on whether the plaintiff can

show that the new window uses the same cone of light, or a substantial part of it, as was used by the old window.

- A plaintiff may have altered his building so much or have so little evidence of the position of the old window that he is unable to prove that he is using the same light as he was using in the old building. In that case, the right would be lost.

Ankerson v Connelly (1907)

The defendant's property originally backed on to a yard. On the ground floor, it had two windows to the yard. At the other end of the yard, there was a shed which was open to the yard and also had a small window on to the plaintiff's premises to the east. The plaintiff's land was separated from the defendant's property by a low wall (the east wall). The defendant pulled down his house and rebuilt a much larger building with two windows on the ground floor in the place of the previous windows. In doing the work, he increased the height of the east wall, retaining a window in the place of the window to the former shed and created two other small windows in the east wall. He also covered over the yard entirely so that the only light to the ground floor windows was that coming through the new openings in the east wall. The alterations destroyed at least three-quarters of the light that the defendant had originally enjoyed. The plaintiff then erected hoardings which substantially interfered with the light to the three windows to the defendant's property. The defendant pulled the hoardings down and the plaintiff commenced proceedings seeking a declaration that the defendant was not entitled to any right to light over the plaintiff's land. The judge awarded the plaintiff a declaration to this effect. The defendant appealed.

The Court of Appeal dismissed the defendant's appeal. The reconstruction and change in character of the defendant's buildings had substantially destroyed the rights to light which he had acquired for the windows in the old building and shed and there was no substantial 'identity' between the old and new buildings. The court considered that the erection of the hoardings would not have entitled the defendant to make a claim prior to his alterations (as the hoardings would not have amounted to a sufficient interference to be actionable) and did not, therefore, entitle him to claim that there had been an actionable interference once his own alterations had blocked out practically the whole of his light.

WH Bailey & Son Ltd v Holborn & Frascati Ltd (1914)

The plaintiffs were the lessees of a property in Oxford Street, London. In 1911, they agreed with an adjoining owner that the latter could carry out building works to its property (known as the 'Gilbert alterations') which would interfere with the plaintiffs' light. The plaintiffs were paid £200 for consenting to the alterations. After these works were carried out, the defendants carried out building works to their property, which also adjoined the plaintiffs' premises. The plaintiffs brought an action for interference with their rights to light. The defendants' defences included an argument that, by consenting to the Gilbert alterations, the plaintiffs had abandoned or lost their right to light over the defendants' property.

The judge held that the plaintiffs had not lost their right to light over the defendants' premises by consenting to the Gilbert alterations. Consent by a dominant owner to a reduction in light coming from one adjoining property, did not mean that he would lose his right to light over other adjoining premises. The judge decided that the defendants' buildings would seriously interfere with the comfortable enjoyment of the plaintiffs' premises, quite apart from the Gilbert alterations, and awarded the plaintiffs damages.

Sometimes alterations to a building will involve changes in the plane or shape of the window or setting back the building from its previous position. Such alterations will not destroy the right to light, provided that there is sufficient coincidence between the original and the new windows. The Court of Appeal in *Scott v Pape* (1886) (see above) considered changes in the plane of windows. The issue was also considered in the following cases.

National Provincial Plate Glass Insurance Co Ltd v Prudential Assurance Co (1877)

The plaintiff and defendant occupied adjacent premises. The plaintiff rebuilt its premises. A room on the ground floor of the old building was lit by a dormer window with three faces, light to which came from a light well between the plaintiff's and the defendant's premises. During the plaintiff's rebuilding works, the dormer window was replaced by a skylight, partially coextensive with the old window, but of a different shape. Subsequently, the defendant commenced rebuilding of its premises. The plaintiff began proceedings claiming (amongst other things) that light through the skylight was obstructed. The defendant argued that the skylight was not the same aperture and was not in the same plane as the original dormer window and, therefore, that the right to light had been lost.

At the trial, the judge considered that the right was not limited to the original dormer window. He also did not consider that the right would be lost by a change of the plane of the window, whether by putting a window in a parallel plane or by putting in a window at an angle to the original window. The judge held therefore that the right to light was not lost by the change from the dormer window to the skylight.

Barnes v Loach (1879)

There was a dispute, on a reference from an arbitrator, as to whether two types of alteration to a row of cottages on the plaintiff's land affected his rights to light over the defendant's land. The first alteration, following resolution of a boundary dispute, was that the walls of a number of cottages, which had projected on to the defendant's land, were moved back onto the plaintiff's land. The windows were the same size and were in the same relative position as the original windows, but they were now set back on to the plaintiff's land. The second alteration was that the occupier of one cottage had built a wall with a new window in it, at a different angle from the original window, outside the original wall. The original window was unaltered.

The court held that the right was not destroyed by the setting back of the wall. A right to light would not be destroyed unless the alteration of the dominant property substantially changed the nature of the property or materially increased the burden on the servient property. The addition of a wall and window outside the original wall and window did not change the nature of the property so substantially as to destroy the right to light.

Bullers v Dickinson (1885)

The frontage of the plaintiff's house originally protruded at an angle into the street (protruding 4 ft at the west and 7 ft 9 in. at the east). The ground floor room was used as a shop and the ground floor front consisted mainly of a shop window. The shop was pulled down in order to allow the widening of the street. A much smaller property was built which did not protrude on to the street. The window in the new property was of a similar size to the old window, but was no longer at an angle to the street and was built 4 ft further back at the west end and 7 ft 9 in. further back at the east end than the original wall. The defendant then constructed a building on the other side of the street and the plaintiff claimed that the defendant's building had interfered with its right to light. The defendant argued that, because the new building was so different from the old and the new room so small, the right to light had been abandoned or lost. However, the judge held that the defendant had failed to prove any intention to abandon the right to light.

4.5.3 Lack of proof of coincidence between new and old windows

Where alterations destroy any coincidence between the old and new windows or where the dominant owner is unable to prove the amount of coincidence between the windows, the right to light may be lost. It is therefore important to keep a careful record of the position of the original windows before demolition.

Pendarves v Monro (1892)

The plaintiffs' new premises had been built on the site of an old pub and house. When the defendant proposed building opposite the plaintiffs' premises, the plaintiffs began an action to prevent the proposed works going ahead. The evidence as to the coincidence of the old and new windows was vague. A witness stated in an affidavit that, to the best of his recollection, the new windows covered in whole or in part the position of the old windows. No plan had been kept. The judge accepted that it was probably right that the present windows covered in part the space occupied by the old windows. But, as he had no evidence of which part(s), he was unable to conclude that some definite part of an old window coincided with some definite part of the new windows. He therefore refused the plaintiffs' application for an interim injunction to prevent the defendant's building proceeding.

News of the World Ltd v Allen Fairhead & Sons Ltd (1931)

The plaintiffs were lessees of premises opposite the defendants' property. Windows in the plaintiffs' premises had the benefit of rights to light over the defendants' premises. However, the plaintiffs then pulled down their property and constructed a new building. No proper plan was drawn up showing the coincidences between the old and new windows and the architect did not have in mind the need to preserve the rights to light. After the plaintiffs' building was rebuilt, the defendants demolished and began to rebuild their own building. The building was designed to be much higher than the original construction. The plaintiffs started an action claiming an injunction and damages for interference with their rights to light. The defendants argued that because the plaintiffs had no intention of preserving the rights to lights on rebuilding, this meant that they should be presumed to have abandoned those rights.

The judge held that a mere lack of evidence of an intention to preserve a right to light was not by itself sufficient to prove an intention to abandon the plaintiffs' rights. However, he also held that above the ground floor the lack of precise evidence as to the identity of the old and new windows made it impossible to hold that any right to light had been retained. On the ground floor, he held that there were substantial coincidences between some new and old windows. However, he found that the plaintiffs had failed to establish a nuisance. He rejected the plaintiffs' argument that they could prove a nuisance by asking the court to disregard all the light coming through the new apertures except those parts which coincided with the old windows. This would mean that the plaintiffs' own acts would have greatly increased the burden on the servient property. The judge also took into account, in rejecting the plaintiffs' claim on the ground floor, the great uncertainty as to the exact dimensions of the old windows.

4.6 EXTINGUISHMENT BY STATUTE

An easement may be extinguished as a result of the compulsory acquisition of land by a local authority in accordance with Part XI of the *Town and Country Planning Act* 1990. Local authorities may compulsorily acquire land in accordance with section 226 of the Act. Section 237 authorises the erection, construction or carrying out or maintenance of any building or work on land acquired or appropriated by a local authority for planning purposes, notwithstanding that it involves interference with an easement. The section applies whether the work is done by the local authority or a subsequent owner of the land. Compensation is payable under section 237(4). The purpose of the section is to facilitate development of land by local authorities by providing that easements (including rights to light) and other rights, which might prevent such development, are overridden and extinguished subject to a right of compensation.

The right to override and extinguish easements is not limited to the initial development carried out on the site, but can include later redevelopments carried out by the local authority or subsequent owners. However, in order to rely on section 237, the development must be related to the 'planning purposes' for which the land was acquired.

Similar provisions exist in Schedule 6 to the *Regional Development Agencies Act* 1998 in relation to the compulsory acquisition of land by a regional development agency. Section 295 of the *Housing Act* 1985 also includes a similar provision that easements will be extinguished when land is acquired for clearance by a local housing authority.

R v City of London Corporation and Royal Mutual Insurance Society ex parte Master and Governors and Commonalty of the Mystery of the Barbers of London (1996)

In the 1950s the Corporation (the local planning authority for the City of London) acquired land for the purpose of redevelopment by compulsory purchase. In 1962, a building lease was granted to the Insurance Society which built Shelley House on the site. Afterwards, in 1969, the Corporation granted land to Barbers and covenanted not to cause any obstruction to the light passing through any of the windows on Barbers' property. In 1995, the Corporation and the Insurance Society agreed to demolish and redevelop Shelley House. This redevelopment would have interfered with Barbers' right to light. Barbers then applied for judicial review of the Corporation's decision that section 237 of the *Town and Country Planning Act* 1990 authorised interference with their right to light. Barbers argued that this section no longer applied once the original development had been carried out and that the right under the Act to interfere with easements did not apply to easements granted by the authority itself.

Barbers' application for judicial review failed. The judge held that where the land had been acquired 'for planning purposes' under the Act, the section was not limited in its application to the original development. The judge stated that, as sites needed to be redeveloped from time to time, a local authority would need to be able to override third party rights when carrying out redevelopments as well as when carrying out the initial development. The judge also held that section 237 was not intended to be limited to rights other than those granted by the local authority itself.

Midtown Ltd v City of London Real Property Company Ltd (2005)

The freehold and leasehold owners of a London office building (the claimants) claimed an injunction or damages against the owner of a neighbouring site (the defendant) on the basis that they had acquired a right to light by prescription with which the defendant's development would substantially interfere. The defendant argued, amongst other things, relying on *R v City of London Corporation* (1996), that it was entitled to interfere with the claimants' rights to light because part of its site had been acquired by the local authority for planning purposes in 1956, as part of the regeneration of London following war damage, and therefore section 237 of the *Town and Country Planning Act* 1990 overrode any right to light. The judge held that the defendant could not rely on section 237. In his view, if a local authority or a subsequent owner wished to rely on the power to override in section 237, the proposed development must be related to the planning purposes for which the land was acquired or appropriated. Otherwise, a developer could rely on this power hundreds of years after the original acquisition when carrying out a development wholly unrelated to the purpose for which the local authority acquired the land. In this case, there was no connection between the defendant's proposed development and the original purpose of the acquisition of the land by the local authority.

Where a right to light is compulsorily overridden by statute, the dominant owner does not have a claim at common law (i.e. a claim in nuisance for interference with the right to light: see Chapter 6 below), but has a statutory claim for compensation. The claim for interference under section 237 of the *Town and Country Planning Act* 1990 is under the *Land Clauses Consolidation Act* 1845 or the *Compulsory Purchase Act* 1965. Claims are made to the Lands Tribunal.

The claim is for diminution in the value of the claimant's land as a result of the loss of the right to light and not the price which the claimant could have demanded for permitting the development (*Wrotham Park Settled Estates v Hertsmere Borough Council* (1993)). Where the development interferes with both windows which have acquired a right to light and other new windows, the claimant is entitled to compensation for all the damage caused to both the old and new windows.

Re London Tilbury and Southend Railway Company and Trustees of Gower's Walk Schools (1889)

The plaintiff demolished a building in respect of which rights to light had been acquired and constructed a new building. Some of the new windows coincided with the original windows. Others occupied entirely different positions. Shortly afterwards, a railway company, in the exercise of its statutory powers erected a warehouse which obstructed light to the plaintiff's building. The plaintiff claimed statutory compensation in relation to all windows which were obstructed. The Court of Appeal decided that, under the

Railways Clauses Act 1845 (which had similar compensation provisions to those applicable to the *Town and Country Planning Act* 1990), the plaintiff was entitled to compensation for the injury both to the old and the new windows. It was impossible to obstruct the new windows, without at the same time obstructing the old windows. Lopes LJ explained that, at common law, the plaintiff would have been entitled to an injunction to prevent obstruction to the windows which had acquired rights to light, which would also have prevented obstruction to the new windows. But, as a result of the legislation, the plaintiff had no such right and was compelled to submit to the obstruction of both the new and old windows. Therefore, the plaintiff was entitled to compensation for the obstruction of both.

Unlike the legislation relating to compulsory purchase, the *Party Walls etc. Act* 1996 specifically provides at section 9 that nothing in the Act will authorise any interference with an easement of light or other easements in or relating to a party wall. Even if a party wall award appears to authorise it, a building owner is not entitled to carry out works which would interfere with a right to light. If a party wall award in fact authorises interference with a right to light, it will not be enforced. The adjoining owner may be able to obtain an injunction to prevent the work going ahead.

Crofts v Haldane (1867)

The defendant had served notice under the then-current party wall legislation and built a wall in accordance with the award of the three surveyors. The plaintiff started proceedings for an injunction claiming that the wall interfered with his right to light. The plaintiff's claim succeeded. The court rejected the argument that the dispute as to the right to light should be determined by the surveyors. The court considered that as the building owner had no right to raise a party wall so as to interfere with the right to light, there was nothing under the Act in relation to which the surveyors could make an award.

5
Infringement of rights to light

5.1 INTRODUCTION

In deciding whether a right to light has been or will be infringed by a neighbouring development, it is necessary to consider:

- the amount of light to which a claimant is entitled;
- tests for infringement (the 45 degree rule and the 50/50 rule);
- other factors, including locality, use and layout of the property, whether the property is residential or commercial, the relevance of artificial light, reflected light and light from other sources; and
- whether the property is entitled to an exceptional amount of light.

5.2 THE AMOUNT OF LIGHT TO WHICH A CLAIMANT IS ENTITLED

A claimant who has acquired a right to light by prescription is entitled to sufficient light, according to the ordinary notions of mankind, for the comfortable use and enjoyment of his house or place of business (as the case may be). Hence, a right to light is not infringed simply because the light is reduced by the construction of a new building on a nearby plot. To amount to an infringement, the light must be reduced beyond that sufficient for the comfortable use and enjoyment of the property. The question therefore is not:

- How much light has been taken and will it reduce the claimant's enjoyment of his property?

The correct question is:

- How much light is left and is that enough for the comfortable use and enjoyment of the property according to people's ordinary requirements?

Colls v Home and Colonial Stores Ltd (1904)

The plaintiffs (Home and Colonial Stores Ltd) were lessees of a building which they used as business premises. On the land opposite, the defendant wished to construct a new building. The plaintiffs began an action claiming an injunction, arguing that the proposed building would interfere with their rights to light. The judge found that, after construction of the defendant's building, the plaintiffs' premises would still be sufficiently lit for all ordinary purposes of occupancy as a place of business. The defendant then constructed the building. However, the Court of Appeal reversed the judge's decision and granted an injunction ordering the defendant to remove the building he had now constructed. The defendant appealed to the House of Lords. On appeal, the issue was whether the plaintiffs, having acquired rights to light under the *Prescription Act*, were entitled at the end of the 20-year prescription period to retain *all* of the light they had enjoyed during that period, without any reduction at all.

The House of Lords reviewed the earlier case law on interference with rights to light. It decided that the right question was whether the plaintiffs had been deprived of so much light as to constitute an actionable nuisance. The words of both Lord Lindley and Lord Davey setting out the House of Lords' decision have often been quoted in subsequent cases:

Lord Davey stated:

> '. . . the owner or occupier of the dominant tenement is entitled to the uninterrupted access through his ancient windows of a quantity of light, the measure of which is what is required for the ordinary purposes of inhabitancy or business of the tenement according to the ordinary notions of mankind.'

Lord Lindley stated:

> '... generally speaking an owner of ancient lights is entitled to sufficient light according to the ordinary notions of mankind for the comfortable use and enjoyment of his house as a dwelling-house, or for the beneficial use and occupation of the house if it is a warehouse, a shop or other place of business.'

The House of Lords held that the wording of the *Prescription Act* (which provides that the right to the access and use of light becomes absolute and indefeasible after the 20-year period) did not change the previous law by entitling a plaintiff to retain *all* the light he had enjoyed during that period. On the facts of the case, the plaintiffs had no cause of action against the defendant.

The decision in *Colls v Home and Colonial Stores Ltd* has stood the test of time. The courts continue to apply the *Colls* 'test' in deciding whether there has been an infringement of a claimant's rights to light. For example, Mummery LJ in the Court of Appeal in *Regan v Paul Properties Ltd* (2007) stated that *Colls*:

> '... is authority for the proposition that the test for infringement of the right to light is whether the obstruction complained of is a nuisance, that is whether there is a substantial loss of light so as to render the occupation of the house less fit for occupation and uncomfortable according to the ordinary notions of mankind. It is not enough for the claimant simply to prove that the light is less than it was.'

Where a right to light has been acquired by express grant, subject to the wording of the grant, it is likely that the amount of light to which the claimant is entitled will also be that set out by the House of Lords in *Colls v Home and Colonial Stores Ltd*: see *Frogmore Developments Ltd v Shirayama Shokusan* (1997) at 2.2.2 above. It is possible to acquire a right to a greater degree of light by prescription or by grant (see 5.5 below).

5.3 TESTS FOR INFRINGEMENT

The test for whether there has been an actionable interference with a claimant's right to light was set out in the decision of

Colls v Home and Colonial Stores Ltd (see 5.2 above). The next question is how a court determines whether there has been an interference.

Over the years, different tests have evolved. The cases refer, in particular, to:

- the 45 degree rule; and
- the 50/50 rule.

5.3.1 The 45 degree rule

An early test adopted by surveyors and the courts was whether the claimant had 45 degrees of unobstructed light left through a particular window, after the defendant's obstruction. This was determined by measuring the angle between the window sill and the top of the proposed/new building. If 45 degrees of unobstructed light remained, it was thought that the claimant had no claim for interference with his right to light. However, early in the 20th century, the courts began to move away from this relatively simplistic approach. The 45 degree rule is now no longer used.

Colls v Home and Colonial Stores Ltd (1904)

Lord Lindley stated that the 45 degree rule was not a rule of law, but that it was generally speaking a 'fair working rule' to consider that no substantial injury was done to a plaintiff where an angle of 45 degrees was left to him, especially if there was good light from other directions as well.

Fishenden v Higgs and Hill Ltd (1935)

The plaintiff was the lessee of a property in Mayfair which he sub-let as flats, retaining the ground floor flat for himself and the basement for a caretaker. On the land opposite, the defendants pulled down their building and started to construct a large block of flats. The plaintiff brought proceedings against the defendants claiming an injunction to restrain them from building so as to interfere with his rights to light. The defendants argued (amongst other things) that if a proposed new building allowed light to the plaintiff's window at an angle of 45 degrees from the perpendicular, the plaintiff could not complain about the reduction in the light in the absence of exceptional circumstances.

The judge decided that the so-called 45 degree rule was not a rule of law or of evidence. There could be no necessary inference that buildings complying with this rule would not cause any interference with light. Each case depended on whether, as a matter of fact and as a question of degree, the defendants' building caused a nuisance to the plaintiff's windows in accordance with the test in *Colls*. He held that the defendants' development would interfere with the plaintiff's rights to light to the ground floor and basement. The Court of Appeal upheld the judge's decision that there would be an actionable interference. Maugham LJ stated that the judge's views on the 45 degree rule were perfectly correct: there was no hard and fast mathematical test involving an angle of 45 degrees.

5.3.2 The 50/50 rule

The 50/50 rule arose from research carried out in the 1920s and 1930s, primarily by Mr Percy Waldram. He devised a more sophisticated method of assessing loss of light than the 45 degree rule. According to the 50/50 rule, an actionable interference arises where, after the defendant's obstruction, less than 50% of the room affected by the obstruction continues to receive an adequate quantity of light. For the purposes of the rule, a room has adequate light if it can receive light from 0.2% of the sky over more than 50% of the room area at a height of 850 mm (the height of a table). The justification for the rule is that an owner would be unreasonable to complain that the corners or other parts of the room where good light is not expected are poorly lit, if the room as a whole remains well lit.

In order to assess the impact of a proposed development on the rooms in a neighbouring building, Waldram diagrams or, nowadays, computer programs, measure the '0.2% contour' in a room before and after the development. It is then possible to calculate the percentage of the room which was well lit before the development and which will remain well lit after the development.

The figure of 0.2% equates to one lumen of light per square foot. Mr Percy Waldram termed this the 'grumble point':

i.e. the point at which an ordinary person would grumble about the amount of light. The 0.2% contour has sometimes been called the 'grumble line'.

In the 1920s, the courts began to use Mr Waldram's research into the 'grumble point' and the 50/50 rule, instead of the 45 degree rule.

Charles Semon & Co v Bradford Corporation (1922)

The plaintiffs were stuff and woollen merchants who had acquired rights to light to their warehouse by prescription. The defendants proposed constructing a building on the opposite side of the street. The plaintiffs claimed that there had been an actionable interference with their rights to light, relying on the fact that the proposed new building would reduce the angle of light to the ground and first floor windows to considerably less than 45 degrees. However, the plaintiffs did not provide any factual or expert evidence about the amount of light which would be left and whether it would be sufficient for the comfortable use of the warehouse. The defendants' expert, Mr Percy Waldram, gave evidence about the 'grumble point' and concluded that, by reference to this, the rooms about which the plaintiffs complained would remain well lit. The judge held, accepting Mr Waldram's evidence, that the rooms would remain well lit after the proposed development.

Hortons' Estate Ltd v James Beattie Ltd (1927)

The plaintiffs were entitled to rights to light over the defendants' property. The defendants proposed to construct a building on their land which would materially diminish the light through a window to a room on the ground floor of the plaintiffs' property. The plaintiffs brought an action claiming an injunction to restrain the defendants from erecting or maintaining any building on their land so as to infringe the plaintiffs' rights to light. The plaintiffs claimed that, even with the development as yet incomplete, the room was inadequately lit for ordinary purposes because, in more than half the room, the light fell below one foot candle (i.e. 0.2% or one lumen per square foot). The defendants argued that, even though the evidence established that their proposed building would leave the room inadequately lit according to ordinary standards, a different standard should be applied to a room situated in a manufacturing town such as Wolverhampton. The judge dismissed the defendants' argument based on locality (see 5.4.1 below) and held, on the basis of the expert evidence as to ordinary standards, that there was an actionable interference.

In 1954, a judge accepted the 50/50 rule as a very rough guide to whether rooms were adequately lit.

William Cory & Son Ltd v City of London Real Property Company Ltd (1954)

The plaintiff owned and occupied an office building in the City of London. The defendant acquired a site on the north, intending to demolish the remaining building on the site and to erect a large office building. The plaintiff claimed an injunction preventing the construction of the new office on the basis that it interfered with its rights to light to the ground and first floors. Expert evidence was given using Waldram diagrams, which showed that the well-lit area of the affected rooms would be reduced to considerably less than 50%. The judge commented that these methods of assessing light had been used by the courts since 1922 and went on to say that:

> 'The practice has been heretofore to say that a room, in which the grumble line comes half way down the room, that is to say, the room is 50 per cent adequately lit and 50 per cent inadequately lit, upon the average is a satisfactory room when required for office use at any rate in a place like the City of London, where it is expected and normal that the electric light will be on at any rate for parts of the room for great parts of the day ... It may be that the standard of light, applying the tests laid down in *Colls'* case, will gradually increase as the years go by. For my part I am today still prepared to accept what has been called the 50-50 rule as a very rough guide as to what rooms are adequately lit.'

He held that the plaintiff had established a case of actionable nuisance and granted an injunction preventing the defendant from building so as to infringe the plaintiff's rights to light.

The 50/50 rule has continued to be generally applied by the courts. Over the years, claimants and defendants in particular situations have argued that it should be disregarded. Nonetheless, the current position based on the case law is that:

- it is a useful guide, although not a rule of law;
- it should not be rigidly applied in all situations, without regard to the size and shape of the rooms and the disposition of light in a room;
- it can be described as a bare or a pretty irreducible minimum; and
- as a result, an actionable interference may occur, in appropriate circumstances, even where more than 50% of the room remains well lit.

Ough v King (1967)

The plaintiff was the owner and occupier of a property in Gravesend. The defendant, a builder, owned the adjoining house. He carried out alterations and built an extension to his property in order to convert it into flats. After the alterations were carried out, the plaintiff complained that he had interfered with light to two windows facing his house to which she had acquired rights to light by prescription. The defendant argued, based on the evidence of his expert (Mr Brian Anstey), that the plaintiff had no claim because, after the development, over 50% of the room (in fact, 51.27%) remained well lit. The defendant argued (relying on *William Cory v City of London Real Property Company Ltd* (1954)) that it was generally accepted that, if half a room at table height was within the area receiving one or more lumens, the room as a whole was regarded as adequately lit, according to the ordinary notions of mankind. The judge held that there had been an actionable interference with the plaintiff's right to light. He stated that he thought that the notions of mankind on the subject of light had changed and were changing: possibly connected with improvement in electric light. He considered that ordinary people would not now accept, for a living room and office on the outskirts of a town like Gravesend, the daylight standard which was accepted 12 years earlier for an office in the City of London (i.e. the office in *William Cory*). The defendant appealed.

The Court of Appeal dismissed the appeal. The judge was entitled to have regard to the locality and to the higher standards expected for comfort as the years went by. Lord Denning was not prepared to regard Mr Waldram's 50/50 rule as a universal rule and considered that in some cases a higher standard might reasonably be required. Diplock LJ stated that there was no rule of law that no one was entitled to more light than one lumen over 50% of a room at table level. He said that the 50/50 rule was considered in the 1920s and, perhaps later, as a convenient rule of thumb. However, the real question was whether the room now received less light than was sufficient according to the ordinary notions of mankind.

Carr-Saunders v Dick McNeil Associates Ltd (1986)

Two windows at the back of the second floor of the plaintiff's property overlooked the defendant's land. A few years after acquiring the property, the plaintiff changed the internal layout of the second floor from offices to open plan. Still later the plaintiff changed the internal layout again, subdividing the second floor into six consulting rooms, two of which were lit by the windows at the rear of the building. The defendant then increased the height of its building and obstructed the access of light to the consulting rooms at the rear of the plaintiff's building. The plaintiff commenced proceedings against the defendant in nuisance, claiming that the defendant had interfered with rights to light acquired under the *Prescription Act*.

The parties' experts produced daylight contour plans and tested the adequacy of the remaining light by using the 50/50 rule. However, they did this on different bases. The defendant's expert treated the room as a single open plan room and calculated that 66.4% of the room received at least one lumen of light at table level before the development and 58.4% did so after the development. He therefore argued that there was no actionable nuisance. The plaintiff's expert measured the subdivided rooms and found that the percentage of the two affected rooms which was well lit fell from 55–57% before the development to 4.5–6.5% afterwards.

The judge rejected the defendant's approach. He considered that it applied the 50/50 rule too rigidly. The justification for the rule was that an owner would be unreasonable to complain that the corners or other parts of the room where good light is not expected are poorly lit. The 50/50 rule:

- was not a rule of law, but merely a useful guide; and
- was not to be applied without any regard to the shape and size of the room or the disposition of the light within the room.

On the facts, the judge decided that, even considering the room as a single open plan room, although overall the light was not reduced below a reasonable standard, it was severely diminished in two of the places where it was reasonably to be expected to be well lit, i.e. near the two rear windows. This left the plaintiff with grounds for dissatisfaction. The subdivision of the second floor reduced the dimensions to which the 50/50 rule was applied and therefore affected the conclusions to be drawn from the rigid application of the rule. The judge went on to consider the need to take into account actual and hypothetical subdivisions of a building (see 5.4.2 below).

Deakins v Hookings (1994)

The plaintiff had acquired a right to light over the defendant's adjoining property. The defendant significantly extended her property. The plaintiff claimed that there was interference with the light to her kitchen and living room and sought an injunction, requiring demolition of part of the defendant's new extension.

In considering whether there had been an actionable interference, the judge reviewed the 50/50 rule. He pointed out that the work of Mr Waldram in the 1920s had led to the belief for many years that there was an almost rigid rule that if half the room was adequately lit (i.e. had not less than one lumen at table level), the light left was sufficient. He considered that the Court of Appeal decision in *Ough v King* (1967), which held that the 50/50 rule was not a rigid rule, did not mean that the rule should be disregarded, but that it should be considered as a bare minimum. The judge made the following important points:

- In a room that was ill-lit, every bit of light was precious.

- Except in an extreme case, it would be difficult to say, once a living room (rather than a store) fell below 50/50, that the light left was adequate.
- In considering a room where more than 50% remained well lit, regard should be had to the use to be made of the remainder and how bad, vis-à-vis that use, the remaining light was.
- The test was not merely a statistical one. The 50/50 test provided a pretty irreducible minimum.

In relation to the living room, the well-lit area had reduced from 51% to 41%. This was the main living room, it was poorly lit to begin with and a drop below 50% pushed it below an acceptable level. The judge took into account, not just the expert evidence, but also the plaintiff's factual evidence and concluded that there was a real and deleterious interference. In relation to the kitchen, the well-lit area had dropped from 88%, but remained over 50%. The judge considered that the affected area could not be used for anything other than circulation, that the area of the room which could be used was adequately lit and concluded that there was no actionable interference.

Midtown Ltd v City of London Real Property Company Ltd (2005)

Separate actions were brought by the freehold and leasehold owners of a property to the west of a site in which the defendant had a long leasehold interest and which it proposed to develop. The claimants asserted that the defendant's proposals would interfere to a substantial degree with their rights to light. They claimed injunctions preventing the defendant from building so as to interfere with their rights to light; alternatively, damages. The judge held that the defendant had infringed the claimants' rights to light, except in relation to one part of the land. In reaching this conclusion, he considered expert evidence of the 0.2% contours for each room and found that the reductions to the available light as a result of the development would be 'very large' and would reduce the light to below 50% well lit. The defendant argued that the time had come to dispense with rigid and unhelpful rules, such as the 50/50 rule, arguing that the existence and use of artificial light should be taken into account. The judge rejected this argument (see 5.4.4 below). After taking into account the principle in *Sheffield Masonic* (1932) (see 5.4.6 below), he concluded that all the relevant rooms would be inadequately lit on the 50/50 test and that the development would amount to a nuisance.

Regan v Paul Properties Ltd (2006)

The claimant was the owner of a maisonette in Brighton. The defendant proposed to construct a development opposite the claimant's property. The claimant started an action claiming that the development would interfere with his rights to light. He claimed an injunction, requiring the defendant to cut back one of the units in the proposed development. The expert evidence was that, prior to the development, the area of the living room which was well lit was 65–67% and that, after the development, it would be reduced to 42–45%. The defendant argued that there was no rule of law that an actionable nuisance was established if the well-lit area fell below 50%.

The judge, having considered the earlier cases, stated that the 50/50 rule was not a rule of law, but that it was a very useful guide which would apply to the majority of cases concerning infringements of rights to light, especially where the dominant property was a residential house and the room in question was a living room, but it need not be followed in exceptional circumstances. In this case, he considered that on a statistical basis (i.e. the reduction to 42–45%), it was plain that there had been an actionable nuisance. He also took into account that the area of the living room which had suffered the loss of adequate light was right in the centre and that it would therefore affect activities carried out in that room. He therefore concluded that the claimant had satisfied the *Colls* test (see 5.2 above). The claimant (successfully) appealed the judge's decision not to award an injunction (see 7.4.2 below). The defendants did not appeal the question of whether there had been an actionable nuisance.

5.4 OTHER FACTORS

There are a number of other factors to be considered in determining whether there has been an actionable interference with a claimant's right to light:

- locality;
- internal use and layout of the property;
- residential or commercial property;
- artificial light;
- reflected light; and
- light from other sources.

5.4.1 Relevance of locality

Courts consider the question of locality in deciding whether there has been a nuisance such as noise or vibration. However, in cases of interference with rights to light, the fact that the claimant's property is in a badly lit area will not reduce the amount of light to which he is entitled to below 50% well lit. In one case, it was unsuccessfully argued that a room in Wolverhampton should be entitled to less light than one in Mayfair. Subsequently, in a case about a building in Mayfair, it was argued (equally unsuccessfully) that less light could be expected in rooms in Mayfair than in other 'more fortunate' districts.

Hortons' Estate Ltd v James Beattie Ltd (1927)

The plaintiffs were entitled to rights to light through windows in their property. The defendants proposed to construct a building on their land which would materially diminish the plaintiffs' light through a window to a room on the ground floor. The plaintiffs brought an action claiming an injunction to restrain the defendants from erecting or maintaining any building on their land so as to infringe the plaintiffs' rights to light. The plaintiffs claimed that, even with the development as yet incomplete, the room was inadequately lit for ordinary purposes because, in more than half the room, the light fell below one foot candle (i.e. 0.2% or one lumen per square foot). The defendants argued that, even though the evidence established that their proposed building would leave the room inadequately lit according to ordinary standards, a different standard should be applied to a room situated in a manufacturing town such as Wolverhampton. They claimed that, even though badly lit, it would be no worse off than other back rooms in the same neighbourhood.

The defendants therefore argued that the plaintiffs had suffered no actionable interference.

The judge disagreed. He held that although buildings in a manufacturing district might be more crowded together than in residential neighbourhoods, the standard of light required to light a room adequately did not vary depending on the location of the premises. He stated that the human eye required as much light for comfortable reading or sewing in Darlington Street, Wolverhampton, as in Mayfair.

Fishenden v Higgs and Hill Ltd (1935)

The plaintiff was a lessee of a property in Mayfair which he sub-let as flats, retaining the ground floor flat for himself and the basement for a caretaker. On the land opposite, the defendants pulled down their building and started to construct a large block of flats. The plaintiff brought proceedings against the defendants claiming an injunction to restrain them from building so as to interfere with his rights to light. The defendants accepted that there would be a substantial reduction in the light. However, they denied that there was an actionable nuisance. The judge held that the defendants' development would interfere with the plaintiff's rights to light to the ground floor and basement. The defendants appealed, arguing (amongst other things) that the judge should have taken into consideration the locality of the plaintiff's premises and the fact that a number of streets in Mayfair received less light than would be left for the plaintiff after the erection of the proposed development.

The Court of Appeal dismissed the defendants' appeal on this issue. It accepted that the question of locality was relevant in claims for nuisance, although Romer LJ considered that it was very much less relevant to cases of loss of light than other nuisances (such as noise and vibration). The court did not accept, however, that whether there was an actionable interference with the plaintiff's right to light should be assessed by reference to the relatively small amount of light received through the windows of a large number of other houses in Mayfair.

On the other hand, it is *possible* that a less crowded area could justify a standard above 50% well lit. This proposition cannot be expressly derived from the case law. However, in 1967 (in *Ough v King*) it was successfully argued that a higher standard of light was applicable to a residential property on the outskirts of Gravesend than that accepted for an office in the City of London in 1954. This justified the finding that there was an actionable interference with a right to light in Gravesend, although 51.27% of the room remained well lit. It needs to be borne in mind that locality was only one of the factors in the case. The other factor, namely increased expectations of light over the years, was at least as important to the decision.

Ough v King (1967)

The plaintiff was the owner and occupier of a property in Gravesend. The defendant, a builder, owned the adjoining house. He carried out alterations to his property which the plaintiff complained interfered with light to two of her windows. The defendant argued that the plaintiff had no claim because, after the development, over 50% of the room (in fact, 51.27%) remained well lit. The judge held that there had been an actionable interference with the plaintiff's right to light. He stated that he thought that the notions of mankind on the subject of light had changed and were changing: possibly connected with improvement in electrical light. He considered that ordinary people would not now accept, for a living room and office on the outskirts of a town like Gravesend, the daylight standard which was accepted 12 years earlier for an office in the City of London (i.e. the office in *William Cory v City of London Real Property Company Ltd* (1954) (see 5.3.2 above)). The defendant appealed.

The Court of Appeal dismissed the appeal. The judge was entitled to have regard to the locality and to the higher standards expected for comfort as the years went by.

5.4.2 Relevance of use and layout of the property

A number of statements of general principle were made by Lord Davey in *Colls v Home and Colonial Stores Ltd* in relation to the use and layout of the dominant property. These have been developed in subsequent cases. Where a right to light has been acquired by prescription, the position can be summarised as follows:

- The light to which the claimant is entitled will not be limited by the use to which he has put a room in the past.
- In determining whether the light received by the claimant's premises has fallen below an acceptable standard, the court will take into account not only the present use and layout of a particular room but also any other arrangement of the space which might reasonably be expected to be adopted in the future.

The position may be different in the case of an express grant of a right to light. In such a case, the claimant's entitlement will depend on the wording of the grant.

Colls v Home and Colonial Stores Ltd (1904)

Lord Davey's statements of principle included:

- A right to light is for access of light to the building and, if the building/windows retain their substantial identity, the easement does not depend on the use made of the rooms and is not varied by any alteration made to the internal structure of the building.
- A person does not lose his right to light by any change in the internal structure of his building or the use to which it is put and regard may be had, not only to the present use, but also to any ordinary uses to which the property is put.

Price v Hilditch (1930)

The plaintiff and defendant owned adjoining properties separated by narrow passages on either side of a dwarf wall on the defendant's land (some 3 ft 9 in. high). The plaintiff had acquired rights to light by prescription for the windows of a kitchen and scullery over the defendant's land. The defendant built an extension on her land and in the course of the works increased the height of the dwarf wall to 23 ft. The plaintiff issued proceedings against the defendant, claiming that the building infringed his rights to light. The defendant argued (amongst other things) that even if the light to the scullery had been interfered with, the plaintiff had failed to establish that there had been an infringement with his rights to light because, after the obstruction, there remained sufficient light for the purposes of the scullery.

The judge found that there had been a significant interference with the light to the scullery, so that it would not be sufficient for the ordinary purposes of occupation of a room in a residential house (in contrast to the ordinary purposes of a scullery). Relying on the comments of Lord Davey in the House of Lords in *Colls* (see above), he decided that the plaintiff's right was not limited by the use to which the room had been put. He therefore held that there was an actionable interference with the right to light to the scullery. However, he did take into account the probability that the scullery would continue to be used as a scullery in deciding to award damages instead of a mandatory injunction to remove the building. The judge rejected the plaintiff's claim in relation to the kitchen.

Carr-Saunders v Dick McNeil Associates Ltd (1986)

Two windows at the back of the second floor of the plaintiff's property overlooked the defendant's land. A few years after acquiring the property, the plaintiff changed the internal layout of the second floor from offices to open plan. Still later the plaintiff changed the internal layout again, subdividing the second floor into six consulting rooms, two of which were lit by the windows at the rear of the building. The defendant then increased the height of its building and obstructed the access of light to the consulting rooms at the rear of the plaintiff's building. The plaintiff commenced proceedings against the defendant in nuisance. The defendant argued that there had been no actionable nuisance because it was not open to a dominant owner to increase the burden on the servient owner by dividing the floor internally into six separate rooms. The defendant maintained that the judge should disregard the internal walls and should treat the second floor as a single room for the purpose of determining whether there was sufficient light.

The calculations of light before and after the development, using the 50/50 rule, varied significantly, depending on whether the room was treated as open plan or subdivided. The judge concluded that the rule should not be rigidly applied without regard to the shape and size of the room and the disposition of light within it (see 5.3.2 above).

The judge went on to consider the need to take into account actual and hypothetical subdivisions of a building and held that three principles must be borne in mind:

- The right acquired by prescription is the right to light to a building as a whole rather than a particular room within it so that the extent of the right is not necessarily to be measured by the internal arrangements of the building.
- The issue in every case is whether there has been a substantial interference with the use and enjoyment of the property, not of a particular room.
- The dominant owner's right to light is not to be measured by the particular use to which the property has been put in the past. The use to which the property has been put does not either increase or reduce the right. The plaintiff was entitled to an amount of light which would leave his premises adequately lit for all ordinary purposes for which they might reasonably be expected to be used. Account must be taken, therefore, not just of the present use but also of the future potential uses of the building.

The judge concluded that it was necessary to consider the effect of the defendant's building works on any other arrangement of the space which might reasonably be expected to be adopted in the future. He held that some subdivision (not necessarily the present subdivision) of the second floor was an ordinary and reasonable use to which the space might be put. There were in fact only two possible subdivisions and, after the development, in both cases the defendants' building would substantially interfere with the light available. He therefore held that the plaintiff had established an actionable nuisance – not on the basis that the present rooms were no longer adequately lit, but because the second floor could no longer conveniently be subdivided in such a way that the subdivided areas each received an adequate amount of light.

Tamares (Vincent Square) Ltd v Fairmont Properties (Vincent Square) Ltd (2007)

The claimant's and defendant's properties were adjacent. The defendant carried out a redevelopment. The claimant claimed that the new building would interfere with the light to four of its ground floor windows: two were the entrance lobby windows and two were by the basement stairs. The entrance lobby windows had been boarded up and the judge held that no right to light had been acquired under the *Prescription Act* in relation to these windows (see 3.4.4 above). However, in case he was wrong in relation to the acquisition point, he then went on to consider whether there was an actionable interference with the light to the entrance lobby windows. There was no interference on the basis of the current arrangement. However, the claimant argued that there could be an interference on the basis of hypothetical alternative arrangements. The hypotheses included the potential demolition and rebuilding of the property or the construction of a bathroom. The judge considered that these hypotheses, which were not based on any satisfactory evidence, were highly speculative and were not therefore reasonably predictable alternative uses. He held that there was no actionable interference with the light to the entrance lobby windows.

5.4.3 Whether the property is residential or commercial

It is often suggested that the courts require a higher standard of light for residential than for commercial properties. This suggestion is frequently based on comments in *Ough v King* (see 5.3.2 above) (where the judge stated that ordinary people would not now accept, for a living room and office on the outskirts of a town like Gravesend, the daylight standard which was accepted 12 years earlier for an office in the City of London and held that there was an actionable interference although the room remained 51.27% well lit) and the perception that an injunction may be more readily awarded in relation to a residential than a commercial property (contrast *Regan v Paul Properties Ltd* (2007) and *Midtown Ltd v City of London Real Property Company Ltd* at 7.4.2 below). However:

- the cases do not expressly state that a higher standard is required for residential property;
- the Court of Appeal upheld the judge's decision in *Ough v King* on the basis of locality and changing standards. It did not expressly rely on the fact that the plaintiff's property was residential;
- the Court of Appeal in *Regan* reviewed the law on final injunctions and made it clear that the *Shelfer* test should be applied. The judge in *Midtown* departed from the

Shelfer test. As explained at 7.4.2 below, it is considered that the Court of Appeal in *Regan* would have been likely to have awarded an injunction if it had heard an appeal on the *Midtown* case.

It is acknowledged that there may be good reasons for insisting on a higher standard of light for residential properties. However, it is submitted that the case law at present does not expressly require it.

5.4.4 Relevance of artificial light

A right to light is a right to natural light. The claimant's ability to use, or practice of using, artificial light is not a defence to an action for interference with a right to light.

Midtown Ltd v City of London Real Property Company Ltd (2005)

The freehold and leasehold owners of a property brought actions against the defendant, who proposed to develop his adjacent site. The claimants asserted that the defendant's proposals would interfere to a substantial degree with their rights to light. Using the 50/50 rule, the defendant's development would reduce the light to below 50% well lit (see 5.3.2 above). However, the offices were habitually lit by artificial light. The defendant argued that this was the modern practice in offices and that the reduction of natural light was irrelevant, if the lighting was actually provided by artificial light. It was argued that the time had come to recognise the real situation and to dispense with rigid and unhelpful rules, such as the 50/50 rule.

The judge rejected the defendant's argument for a number of reasons:

- It would mean that there would never be a successful challenge to an infringement of light because it could always be said, no matter how much actual light was taken away, that it was possible to fill the gap with artificial light.
- It undermined the potential advantages in particular cases of natural light over artificial light.

- It failed to take account of potential future uses of the site. Redevelopment could involve greater use of natural light.
- Whilst other owners in the City might have been prepared to give up their rights to natural light, it would not be appropriate to require an owner's rights to be bargained away against his wishes.

Nonetheless, the judge did take into account the use of artificial light as a factor in deciding not to award an injunction to the leasehold owners of the property (but see 7.4.2 below, where doubts are expressed about the approach taken in the judgment to the granting of injunctions). It is suggested that the refusal of an injunction on the basis that artificial light is used by a claimant would effectively require the claimant's rights to be bargained away, which would be contrary to the last of the judge's reasons set out above.

Tamares (Vincent Square) Ltd v Fairmont Properties (Vincent Square) Ltd (2007)

The claimant's and defendant's properties were adjacent. The defendant carried out a redevelopment. The claimant claimed that the new building would interfere with the light to four of its ground floor windows: two were the entrance lobby windows and two were by the basement stairs. A right to light had been acquired in relation to the basement staircase windows. In considering whether there had been an actionable interference with the right to light to these windows, the judge held (on the basis of *Midtown*) that he had to ignore the fact that, in a relatively modern office block, the artificial lights might well be on the whole time, although he stated that he could bear it in mind on the question of remedy. He concluded that there was a real injury (i.e. an actionable interference with the right to light), although in the 'real world' situation of artificial light, he considered that the complaint was a trivial one.

5.4.5 Relevance of reflected light

In addition to direct natural light, a room may sometimes benefit from reflected light from the (defendant) servient owner's building. This could happen if light reflects off glazed tiles on that building. A court will not take such light into account in deciding whether there has been an infringement of a claimant's right to light. The reason for this is that the dominant owner has no control over the light-reflecting material on the servient owner's land: for example, he cannot prevent the servient owner from removing the tiles.

Dent v Auction Mart Company (1866)

The plaintiffs were the freehold and leasehold owners of two properties. The defendant bought houses backing on to the plaintiffs' properties and proposed to rebuild these considerably higher and closer to the boundaries with the plaintiffs' properties. The plaintiffs claimed injunctions preventing the defendant from interfering with their rights to light. The defendant argued that the loss of light might be remedied by the use of white enamelled tiles and was willing to face the back wall of the development with such tiles. The judge rejected this argument, saying that it was quite preposterous for a defendant to say: 'Let us damage you, provided we apply such and such a remedy'. He pointed out that a person who wished to preserve his light had no power to compel his neighbour to preserve the tiles, or a mirror (which might be better) or to keep them clean. Nor would he have covenants which he could enforce against future owners to compel them to do this.

Price v Hilditch (1930)

The plaintiff and defendant owned adjoining properties separated by narrow passages on either side of a dwarf wall on the defendant's land (some 3 ft 9 in. high). The plaintiff had acquired rights to light by prescription for the windows of a kitchen and scullery over the defendant's land. The defendant built an extension on her land and in the course of the works increased the height of the dwarf wall to 23 ft. The plaintiff issued proceedings against the defendant, claiming that the building infringed his rights to light.

The judge found that there had been a significant interference with the light to the scullery, so that it would not be sufficient for the ordinary purposes of occupation of a room in a residential house. He held that he was not entitled to take into account the fact that some reflected light came over the top of the plaintiff's building on to the new wall and was reflected back from the new wall into the scullery. He considered that the continuance of this reflected light depended on, for example, whether the defendant chose to put a trellis or a creeper on the wall. In such cases, there was nothing that a plaintiff could do to compel the defendant to maintain the reflective surface. In any event, reflected light was a different kind of light from that to which a plaintiff was entitled by prescription.

Deakins v Hookings (1994)

The plaintiff had acquired a right to light over the defendant's adjoining property. The defendant significantly extended her property. The plaintiff claimed that there was interference with the light to her kitchen and living room and sought a final mandatory injunction, requiring demolition of part of the defendant's new extension. The wall of the defendant's property facing the plaintiff's property was faced in white brick and white plastic in order to mitigate the effect on the plaintiff's light. The judge held that the relevant question was whether there had been interference with direct light and that a special arrangement by the servient owner to ensure a degree of reflection (by colouring the wall white) would not assist as there was no certainty that this could be maintained in the future.

Sheffield Masonic Hall Company Ltd v Sheffield Corporation (1932)

In this case, which dealt with the account to be taken of natural light received from other sources (see 5.4.6 below), the judge made some comments, which did not form part of the actual decision in the case, about the use of reflected light. He considered that reflected or diffused light coming into the premises, which was not connected with the defendant, should be taken into account in considering whether the light had been reduced beyond that sufficient for the comfortable use and enjoyment of the property.

5.4.6 Relevance of natural light received from other sources

In considering whether or not there has been an actionable interference with a right to light, the court may take into consideration natural light received by the premises from other sources. However, this is subject to two caveats.

First, light in respect of which the claimant has no right to light should not be taken into account.

Colls v Home and Colonial Stores Ltd (1904)

Lord Lindley in the House of Lords pointed out that light from other quarters should not be disregarded in deciding whether there has been an interference with the plaintiff's right to light, but that light to which a right has not been acquired by grant or prescription, and of which the plaintiff may be deprived at any time, ought not to be taken into account.

Jolly v Kine (1907)

Lord Atkinson in the House of Lords stated that, in determining whether or not the quantity of light which the dominant owner would continue to enjoy would be sufficient, regard could only be had to the light which that owner is by grant or prescription legally entitled to enjoy. Light which could with impunity be obstructed and windows which could at any time be almost entirely blocked up or altogether darkened, must be excluded from consideration.

Secondly, where a building has rights to light through windows on two sides, the adjacent owner on one side cannot build as high as he likes, relying on the fact that light will continue to be received through windows on the other side. One adjacent owner may only build to such a height as will leave sufficient light for the dominant owner, if and when a similar building is constructed by the owner on the other side.

Sheffield Masonic Hall Company Ltd v Sheffield Corporation (1932)

The plaintiff and defendant owned commercial properties on the opposite sides of Surrey Street. The plaintiff's dining room contained a number of windows, one of which had acquired a right to light by prescription over the defendant's property. The dining room also had a right to light through windows overlooking Eyre Street. At the time, there was only a low building on Eyre Street opposite the plaintiff's property. The land on Eyre Street was owned by a third party. The defendant began to increase the height of his building. The plaintiff claimed that the height of the defendant's new building interfered with his right to light. The defendant argued that it could build as high as it wished, relying on the fact that the plaintiff's room received light from another source.

The judge rejected the defendant's argument. Applying common sense, the judge held that the proper view was that the defendant could build to such a height as, with a similar building by the third party, would leave sufficient light for the plaintiff. The judge found that, taking this into account, the defendant's building did not leave the plaintiff's room with enough light for the ordinary purposes of its use either, as at present, as a dining room or for other purposes for which it might be used in the future. The judge accordingly awarded the plaintiff damages.

Midtown Ltd v City of London Real Property Company Ltd (2005)

In this case (see 5.3.2 above), the claimants' property had the benefit of light from two sides. The defendant accepted that the principle in *Sheffield Masonic* (1932) applied. Taking this into account would mean that all the affected rooms were less than 50% well lit. The judge therefore found that there had been an actionable nuisance.

Tamares (Vincent Square) Ltd v Fairmont Properties (Vincent Square) Ltd (2007)

In this case (see 5.4.2 above), the claimant brought an action for interference with the light to four of its ground floor windows: two were the entrance lobby windows and two were by the basement stairs. Amongst other things, the claimant argued that there was an actionable interference as a result of the *Sheffield Masonic* principle. The defendant's evidence was that, if a building of the same size as its new building were erected on the square owned by a third party adjoining owner, this would not make any material difference to the light through the claimant's ground floor windows. However, the claimant argued that the hypothetical building should be placed closer to its property than the square: in effect up to the middle of the current road, as the presumption was that the adjoining owner's land extended to the middle line of the road. The judge decided that it was a very remote possibility that the square would ever be built on and dismissed the argument that the building should extend to the middle of the road as a far-fetched and utterly remote possibility. He did not accept that the principle in *Sheffield Masonic* required consideration of such a remote possibility. In any event, he held that there was insufficient evidence that the construction of a building in such a location would cause an actionable nuisance.

5.5 RIGHT TO AN EXCEPTIONAL QUANTITY OF LIGHT

Buildings are capable of acquiring a right to an exceptional quantity of light by prescription and by grant. The extent of a right to light made by express grant will depend upon the words used in the grant.

Allen v Greenwood (1980)

The plaintiffs' greenhouse had been in use for over 20 years as a domestic greenhouse when the defendants parked a caravan and constructed a close-boarded fence next to it, both of which obstructed the light it received. The obstruction reduced the access of light to the greenhouse to such an extent that it could no longer be used to grow plants, although it could have been used to read a book. The defendants argued that only an ordinary (and not an extraordinary) amount of light could be acquired by prescription. They also argued that the right to light was for the purposes of illumination only and not a right to the direct rays of the sun, to heat or to other beneficial properties from the sun's rays.

The Court of Appeal held that the plaintiffs were entitled to the amount of light necessary to use the greenhouse. First, the right was to be measured in accordance with the nature of the building and the purpose for which it was used. Where a building (such as a greenhouse) requires a high degree of light, for its ordinary use, that high degree of light is an ordinary amount of light for that type of building. Secondly or alternatively, it held that an exceptional or especially high degree of light could be acquired by prescription after 20 years' use, to the knowledge of the servient owners. The Court of Appeal also dismissed the defendants' argument that the right to light was for the purposes of illumination only. It accepted the plaintiffs' argument that they were entitled, by virtue of their prescriptive right to light, to all the benefits of the light, including the rays of the sun, and that warmth was an inseparable product of daylight. Goff LJ cautioned that the position might be different where there was a question of solar heating and that, in such a case, it might be right to separate the heat, or some other property of the sun, from its light.

6
Causes of action and parties

6.1 INTRODUCTION

Before bringing a claim in relation to infringement of a right to light, it is necessary to consider:

- the legal basis of the claim (the cause of action); and
- the parties (the claimant(s) and defendant(s)).

6.2 CAUSE OF ACTION

The cause of action for infringement of an easement, including a right to light, is private nuisance. Nuisance is a tort. Where a party has the benefit of a restrictive covenant (e.g. a covenant prohibiting an adjacent owner from building in a way which would interfere with his neighbour's rights to light), he may also have a cause of action for breach of the restrictive covenant.

The remedies available in rights to light cases are discussed in Chapter 7. Claims, depending on their value, may be brought in the High Court or County Court.

6.3 PARTIES

Two issues arise in relation to the parties to an action:

- Who can sue (claimants)?
- Who can be sued (defendants)?

6.3.1 Who can sue (claimants)?

A claim in nuisance can be made by a person with an interest in land. This is because nuisance is a claim relating to a person's use and enjoyment of land. Therefore, claims can be made by:

- freeholders, leaseholders/tenants who are in actual occupation of the land;
- reversioners (i.e. owners not in occupation), if damage is caused to the reversion; and
- licensees with exclusive possession of the land.

In addition, the decision of *Foster v Warblington UDC* (1906) established an exception for someone in exclusive possession of land even if he could not prove his title to (i.e. interest in) the land. Claims cannot be made by others sharing a property, but who do not have an interest in the land, e.g. children, friends and au pairs.

Generally, in rights to light cases, the claimant will be the freehold or leasehold owner of the property, i.e. the party who has acquired a right to light.

Hunter v Canary Wharf Ltd (1997)

This was not a rights to light case, but is the leading case (a decision of the House of Lords) on the question of who can sue in nuisance. The plaintiffs occupied properties in the London Docklands area. There were approximately 690 of them. They included freeholders, tenants, spouses, partners, children and other relatives. They started two actions in relation to the construction of Canary Wharf. In the first action, they claimed for negligence and nuisance arising out of the construction of Canary Wharf Tower, which they alleged had interfered with their television reception. In the second action, they claimed for negligence and nuisance arising out of dust from the construction of a link road. One of the issues in the actions was whether all the plaintiffs had a right to sue for nuisance. This issue reached the House of Lords on appeal.

The House of Lords held that an action in private nuisance is brought in relation to interference which affects a plaintiff's enjoyment of his rights over the land. Lord Goff explained that since the tort of nuisance is a tort relating to the plaintiff's enjoyment of his rights over land:

- an action in nuisance will usually be brought by the person in actual possession of the land (as freeholder, tenant or as licensee with exclusive possession); although

- a reversioner (an owner not in possession of the land) may sue in respect of a nuisance of a sufficiently permanent character to damage his reversion; and
- as an exception, a person who is in exclusive possession of the land may sue, even if he cannot prove his title to the land. This was a reference to the exception established in *Foster v Warblington UDC* (1906).

The claims of those plaintiffs without a sufficient interest in the land therefore failed.

Butcher Robinson & Staples Ltd v London Regional Transport (2000)

The claimants brought an action against the defendant in private nuisance and negligence for disturbance, noise and vibration. The claimants were a number of companies, all separate legal entities, which were 100% owned subsidiaries of a company called Chapter Group plc (CG). CG owned the freehold of two properties, which were affected by works for the Jubilee Line extension carried out by the defendant over a four-year period. The claimants all occupied CG's premises. There were no leases or licences between CG and the companies. There was a trial of a preliminary issue as to whether the claimants had sufficient proprietary interest in the property to maintain an action in nuisance or negligence. The claimants argued that they should be considered as tenants or licensees with exclusive possession of parts of the premises, which resulted in them collectively having exclusive possession of the whole of the premises.

The arrangements as to occupation of the premises involved reallocation of rooms from month to month and a lack of clarity as to which parts of the property were allocated to which claimant at any particular time. The judge held that this did not give rise to rights of exclusive possession, whether by tenancy or licence, which were enforceable at law. Even if the claimants had had the right to exclusive possession of some parts of the premises, these parts did not make up the whole of the premises as there were common parts, vacant parts and the Chairman's office which were excluded from the claimants' possession. Applying the principles set out in *Hunter v Canary Wharf Ltd* (1997), the judge held that an action in private nuisance only extended to a claimant who had a right to exclusive possession of the land, that the claimants did not have exclusive possession and, therefore, had no sufficient interest in the land to bring an action in private nuisance.

As set out above, the House of Lords in *Hunter v Canary Wharf Ltd* (1997) made it clear that reversioners (i.e. owners, not in possession of the property) may have a claim for damage to their interest in the property (known as the reversion). In rights to light cases, the damage to the reversion may be diminution in value of, and structural damage to, the premises. The cases show that where both the lessee/leasehold owner (who is in occupation of the premises) and the reversioner (who is not) suffer damage as a result of the nuisance, both have claims.

Jesser v Gifford (1767)

The plaintiff had a reversionary interest in a property with rights to light over the defendant's land. The windows were obstructed by a wall constructed by the defendant on his land. The plaintiff brought an action in respect of the interference. The defendant argued that, as the plaintiff was not in possession of the property, but was merely a reversioner, he had an insufficient interest in the property to bring a claim.

The court found in favour of the plaintiff. The plaintiff reversioner had a sufficient interest in the property because, if he wanted to sell the property, the defendant's obstruction would reduce the value of the property. The court held that in such circumstances, an action could be brought both by the person in possession of the property and the reversioner for the loss suffered by each.

Shelfer v City of London Electric Light Co (1895)

An electric lighting company (the defendant) erected powerful engines near to property, owned by the plaintiffs in one action (the reversioners) and leased to the plaintiff in the second action. Owing to excavations for the foundations of the engines and to vibration and noise from the engines when installed, structural damage was caused to the house and annoyance and discomfort to the lessee. In addition, the defendant intended substantially to increase the engine power in the future. The plaintiffs started actions for injunctions to stop the defendant's engines and to prevent the defendant from continuing to damage the plaintiffs' property and for damages.

The Court of Appeal considered (amongst other things) whether the plaintiff reversioners could bring an action for private nuisance against the defendant. It held that reversioners could only bring such an action where the reversion itself was affected by the nuisance. It considered that the structural damage and cracks in the walls were evidence of serious and permanent injury to the reversion. The reversioners were therefore entitled to bring an action against the defendant. They were awarded an injunction and were also entitled to damages for past damage to the property.

Midtown Ltd v City of London Real Property Company Ltd (2005)

Actions were brought by the freehold and leasehold owners of a property to the west of a site in which the defendant had a long leasehold interest and which it proposed to develop. The claimants asserted that the defendant's proposals would interfere to a substantial degree with their rights to light. They claimed a final prohibitory injunction preventing the defendant from building so as to interfere with their right to light or damages, in the alternative. The premises were occupied by the claimant leasehold owner. The claimant freehold owner had only a financial interest in the premises.

The judge held that the defendant had infringed the claimants' rights to light, except in relation to one part of the land. The judge refused both the freeholder and the leaseholder an injunction (see 7.4.2 below). In relation to the freeholder, in deciding not to award an injunction, the judge took into account that it was only interested in the property from a money making point of view and, therefore, that if the value of the property had been diminished, this could be compensated by money. He, nonetheless, held that both the freehold and leasehold owners were entitled to damages for infringement of their rights to light.

An exception to the rule requiring a claimant to have an interest in the land before he can sue for nuisance was provided by the case of *Foster v Warblington UDC* (1906). This exception is limited and exists where there is no doubt that the claimant has exclusive possession of the property, but he is unable to prove his ownership of it.

Foster v Warblington UDC (1906)

The plaintiff had bought oyster ponds (used for the storage of oysters to be fattened for sale) on the foreshore some 25 years before the action and the ponds had been used by his predecessors for many years before that. The plaintiff brought an action against the defendant Council in nuisance and trespass for polluting the oyster ponds by discharge of sewage. The defendant argued, amongst other things, that the plaintiff had no sufficient interest in the land (i.e. the soil of the foreshore on which the oyster ponds were situated) to give him a right to sue. It was not clear to whom the soil belonged legally or whether the plaintiff had acquired title to it, for example, by adverse possession. The Court of Appeal held that the plaintiff had a right to sue, as exclusive occupier of the ponds, whether or not he had acquired an interest in the land itself.

6.3.2 Who can be sued (defendants)?

A party is liable for a nuisance (including interference with rights to light) if he has created, adopted or continued it. Potential defendants in rights to light cases include the original creator of the nuisance, the freehold owner and the leasehold owner of the premises.

6.3.2.1 Creating the nuisance

A claimant may wish to bring an action against the party who originally created the nuisance, whether or not he is the owner of the property. In straightforward cases, this will simply be an action against the owner of the servient premises. However, the nuisance may have been created by a party who has disposed of his interest in the premises or who did not have any interest in the servient premises. For centuries, it has been established that a party who, having created a nuisance, subsequently disposes of the property, remains liable for the consequences of the nuisance. Similarly, a party is liable for creating a nuisance, whether or not he is the owner of the land on which the nuisance is created.

Rosewell v Prior (1701)

The plaintiff owned a house with rights to light over the adjoining land. The defendant was a yearly tenant of the adjoining land and he constructed a building on that land which interfered with the plaintiff's rights to light. The plaintiff successfully brought one action against the defendant for infringement of his rights to light. After the action, the defendant did not remove the offending buildings and instead subleased the premises to a third party. After this, the plaintiff brought a second action against the defendant for continuing the obstruction. The court held that it was a fundamental principle that the person who created the wrong (in this case, erected the offending building) was responsible for all consequential damage.

Thompson v Gibson (1841)

The plaintiff owned a marketplace. The defendants superintended and directed the construction of a building on land belonging to the Corporation of Kendal (of which the defendants were members). Once constructed, the building obstructed part of the plaintiff's marketplace and excluded the public from that area. The plaintiff brought an action against the defendants for continuing the nuisance. The court held that because the defendants had created the nuisance they continued to be liable for the consequences, regardless of the fact that they had no interest in the land on which the obstruction had been built. The judge used the example of a rights to light case, saying that the person who originally erected a wall obstructing windows would not be liable only to pay the first day's loss, but would continue to be liable for as long as the consequences of his wrongful act continued and would have to pay damages for the whole period. In this case, the fact that the defendants were not entitled to go on to the plaintiff's land to remove the nuisance without also being guilty of trespass was a consequence of their original wrong; and they could not now use this to excuse themselves from paying damages for the injury they had caused.

6.3.2.2 Continuing or adopting the nuisance

A claimant may also be able to bring an action against an owner of land, who did not create the nuisance (in the case of rights to light, the obstruction), but has adopted or continued it. The case law in this area does not specifically relate to rights to light, but the principles are applicable to such cases.

Sedleigh-Denfield v O'Callaghan (1940)

The defendant college and the plaintiff owned adjoining premises. The council fitted pipes into a ditch on the defendant's land to supply water to nearby flats. The defendant was not informed by the council about the existence of the pipes on its land. The defendant did, however, employ someone to check its land twice a year and the employee became aware of the pipes. In fitting the pipes, the council failed to fix a guard over the ditch to prevent it becoming blocked by debris. Three years later the ditch became blocked and the plaintiff's land was flooded. The plaintiff brought proceedings in nuisance against the defendant for damages.

The House of Lords held that the defendant was liable in damages for the nuisance which it had continued and adopted. It held that an occupier *continued* a nuisance if, in circumstances in which he knew or should have known of its existence, he failed to take any reasonable means to bring it to an end, although he had ample time to do so. A person *adopted* a nuisance if he made any use of the thing (e.g. a building) which constituted the nuisance. In this case, the defendant college had allowed the nuisance to continue, by failing to put a grid on the ditch to prevent it becoming blocked. It had also adopted the nuisance, by using the pipe for getting rid of water from their property without making it safe.

6.3.2.3 Action against freehold or leasehold owner

Where the servient property is leased, a claimant will also need to decide whether to bring an action against the freehold owner (landlord) or the lessee (tenant). In some cases, it may be possible to sue either. However, this is not always the case. For example:

- a court will not order a mandatory injunction against a tenant to pull down buildings belonging to the landlord which infringe the plaintiff's rights to light, where the landlord is not a party to the action; and
- a tenant may not be liable for obstructions caused prior to his tenancy which he has no power to abate.

Barnes v Allen (1927)

The freehold owner of no. 11 leased it to the defendant for a period of ten years. Number 10 was owned and occupied by the plaintiff. The plaintiff's property had rights to light over no. 11. With the consent of the freeholder, the defendant partially demolished the leased property and constructed new buildings on the land of greater height and width. The new buildings obstructed some of the plaintiff's windows. The plaintiff claimed a mandatory injunction against the defendant requiring it to pull down the new buildings. The judge held that where the freeholder was not a party to the action, a mandatory injunction could not be granted against the defendant lessee of the servient property. The effect of the injunction would be to order the lessee to pull down property belonging to his landlord. The court could not make an order for an injunction, unless the defendant was in a position to comply with it. As it was not the defendant's property, and the court was in no position to bind the freeholder because he was not party to the proceedings, no mandatory injunction was made.

Ryppon v Bowles (1615)

The plaintiff owned a property with a right to light over property owned by Mr Henson. Mr Henson constructed new buildings on his land (in place of the original shed) which completely obstructed one of the plaintiff's windows. Mr Henson then leased the new buildings to the defendant. The plaintiff brought an action against the defendant in respect of the obstruction. The Chief Justice decided that a plaintiff could not claim against a tenant who had no power to remove the obstruction. If the plaintiff in this action had any remedy for the obstruction, he should have claimed it against the freeholder, Mr Henson.

A landlord will not always be liable for interference with rights to light caused by the tenant. For example, where a tenant proposes to construct a building which would interfere with an adjacent owner's rights, a court will not order an injunction against the landlord restraining him from interfering with those rights, when he is unable to take any further action as a result of having granted the lease.

Celsteel Ltd v Alton House Holdings Ltd (1986)

The lessor (the first defendant) owned a multi-storey block of flats. It had granted a 99-year lease of a large part of the ground floor to an oil company (the second defendant). The lease authorised the oil company to build a car wash. The plaintiffs were lessees from the first defendant of flats in the same block and had a right of way to their garages on the ground floor. They brought an action against both the lessor and the oil company, claiming injunctions against both defendants preventing them from blocking the right of way by constructing the car wash. The Court of Appeal decided that the judge had been wrong to order an injunction against the lessor, restraining it from interfering with the plaintiffs' right of way. This was because, having granted the 99-year lease, the lessor had no power to interfere any further with the plaintiffs' right of way by the construction of the car wash.

7
Remedies

7.1 INTRODUCTION TO REMEDIES

There are a number of remedies available to a person who establishes that there has been an actionable interference with his rights to light. Those remedies are:

- abatement (self-help);
- declaratory relief;
- injunction; and
- damages.

7.2 ABATEMENT

Abatement is a self-help remedy. A person who suffers a nuisance is entitled to enter his neighbour's property and put an end to, or abate, the nuisance. Centuries ago, it was permissible for a person to exercise this remedy in a variety of cases where easements, including rights to light, had been infringed.

R v Rosewell (1699)

The defendant had gone on to the plaintiff's land and pulled down part of his house on the basis that it interfered with his rights to light. The court stated that:

> 'If H. builds a house so near mine that it stops my lights, or shoots the water upon my house, or is in any other way a nuisance to me, I may enter upon the owner's soil and pull it down ...'

However, the modern legal position is different. The remedy of abatement is now only available in simple cases, such as an overhanging branch or an encroaching tree root, which would not justify the expense of legal proceedings, or in urgent cases. The remedy cannot be used where the claimant has tried and failed to obtain an injunction to remove the nuisance.

Burton v Winters (1993)

The plaintiff began proceedings complaining that the defendants' garage encroached on the plaintiff's property. Due to the small amount of the encroachment (some 4.5 in.), the judge refused to award an injunction requiring the defendants to take down the garage. The plaintiff subsequently built a wall on the defendants' land in front of the garage and rebuilt it, when the defendants took it down. Even after the defendants had obtained an injunction preventing her from trespassing on their land and from wrongly interfering with their property, the plaintiff made a hole in the roof of the garage and took a sledgehammer to its walls. As this was a breach of the injunction, she was committed to prison for contempt.

The Court of Appeal dismissed the plaintiff's appeal. It held that the right to abate the nuisance or to remove a trespass was confined to simple cases such as an overhanging branch, or an encroaching root, which would not justify the expense of legal proceedings, and to urgent cases which required immediate remedy. Where, as here, the plaintiff had applied for a mandatory injunction (to compel the defendants to remove the garage) and failed, the sole justification for the self-help remedy had gone. In her original action for trespass and nuisance, the court had decided that the plaintiff was not entitled to have the wall removed. It therefore followed that she had no right to remove it herself.

7.3 DECLARATIONS

If there is a dispute or uncertainty as to a party's rights, he may wish to apply to court for a declaration. Such situations may include whether a right to light has been acquired; whether a right to light has been abandoned; or how a deed should be construed. A declaration as to a party's rights may be claimed in the same action as an injunction and damages.

Ankerson v Connelly (1907)

The defendant made very significant alterations to his property which destroyed at least three-quarters of the light that he had previously enjoyed. The plaintiff then erected hoardings which substantially interfered with the light to the windows to the defendant's property. The defendant pulled the hoardings down and the plaintiff commenced proceedings seeking a declaration that the defendant was not entitled to any right to light over the plaintiff's land. The judge awarded the plaintiff a declaration to this effect. The Court of Appeal dismissed the defendant's appeal on the basis that the reconstruction and change in character of the defendant's buildings had substantially destroyed the rights to light which he had acquired for his original windows and that there was no substantial 'identity' between the old and new buildings (see 4.5.2 above).

7.4 INJUNCTIONS

Where a party is concerned that building work will infringe or has already infringed his rights to light and wants the work to be stopped or a building to be removed, he will need to consider applying to court for an injunction.

There are two types of injunction:

- *Prohibitory* injunctions are court orders preventing a party from commencing or continuing work which would interfere with his neighbour's rights to light.
- *Mandatory* injunctions are court orders requiring a party to carry out a positive act, such as removing work that has already been done.

Injunctions can be obtained either:

- on an interim basis; or
- on a final basis.

Interim injunctions (which were known as interlocutory injunctions prior to the introduction of the *Civil Procedure Rules* 1998) can be obtained quickly, particularly if the situation is urgent. Interim injunctions, because they are made at an early stage and on the basis of limited evidence, are temporary only. An interim injunction stopping building work will generally last until the trial of the action, at which stage the court will decide whether to grant a final injunction.

7.4.1 Interim injunctions

The purpose of an interim injunction is to protect the claimant's rights pending the trial. Interim injunctions are ordered at an early stage of court proceedings. They can be ordered on very short notice in an urgent situation and in such a situation, if necessary, the application can be made without notice (i.e. without informing the defendant in advance). Interim injunctions are temporary measures. If granted without the opportunity for the defendant to make submissions, the injunction will last until a further hearing at which both parties are able to present evidence and arguments. If granted after hearing argument and evidence from both sides, interim injunctions will usually last until the trial of the action.

The court makes a decision on an interim injunction after seeing some evidence, but inevitably less than would be available at trial, and without cross-examination. Therefore, in order to protect the defendant, who may be prevented by an injunction from continuing with his building development, the claimant will almost always be obliged to give an 'undertaking in damages' (also called an 'undertaking as to damages'). This means that the claimant agrees that, if at trial it is established that he was not entitled to an injunction, he will pay any damages that the defendant suffers as a result of the interim injunction. These could include the costs of delay to the development and could, in the case of a large commercial development, amount to a significant amount of money.

Interim injunctions may be either prohibitory or mandatory (as to which, see 7.4 above).

7.4.1.1 Prohibitory interim injunctions

The principles on which courts award prohibitory interim injunctions were set out in the House of Lords' decision in the case of *American Cyanamid Co v Ethicon* (1975). This was not a rights to light case, but the principles are applicable to, and are applied in, rights to light cases.

American Cyanamid Co v Ethicon (1975)

The House of Lords set out a three-stage test for the granting of an interim injunction. Before granting an injunction:

- the court must be satisfied that there is a serious question to be tried, i.e. the claim must not be frivolous or vexatious;
- the court must consider the adequacy of damages. This involves two steps:
  - first, the court must consider whether, if the plaintiff were to succeed at trial, damages would be an adequate remedy. If damages would be an adequate remedy and the defendant would be in a financial position to pay them, no interim injunction should normally be granted, and
  - secondly, the court must consider whether, if the defendant were to succeed at trial, he would be adequately compensated by the plaintiff's undertaking in damages for the loss caused by being prevented from carrying out the work between the time of the application for the interim injunction and the trial. If he would be adequately compensated, then an interim injunction should be granted;
- if there is doubt as to the adequacy of damages to the claimant or the defendant, the court must consider the 'balance of convenience'. In doing this, it will take into account any factors relevant to the facts of the case. If other factors are evenly balanced, then the court should preserve the status quo. For example, if the building works have not been started, preserving the status quo will involve granting an injunction to prevent them being carried out.

Often applications for interim injunctions are agreed without a contested hearing on the basis that the defendant agrees to give an undertaking to the court not to carry out any further building works. In such cases, the claimant will usually, in return, give an undertaking in damages. This is what happened in *Regan v Paul Properties Ltd* (2006).

Regan v Paul Properties Ltd (2006)

The claimant was the owner of a maisonette in Brighton. He claimed that the defendant's development would infringe his rights to light and applied for an interim injunction. Instead of an injunction, the defendant agreed to provide an undertaking not to increase the height of the buildings before the conclusion of the trial. In return, the claimant gave an undertaking in damages. The claimant then went on to claim a final mandatory injunction (see 7.4.2 below). The defendant also tried to enforce the claimant's undertaking in damages (see 7.4.1.3 below).

7.4.1.2 Mandatory interim injunctions

A court may, in the exercise of its discretion, award a mandatory interim injunction. This is an injunction which forces the defendant to take a positive step, such as removing part of a building obstructing the claimant's light. It is generally considered that a mandatory interim injunction carries a greater risk of injustice if it turns out to have been wrongly granted than a prohibitory interim injunction, which does not require such a drastic step as taking down a building. Therefore, the test for whether a mandatory interim injunction should be granted is slightly stricter than that for the grant of a prohibitory injunction (as to which, see 7.4.1.1 above).

Nottingham Building Society v Eurodynamics Systems (1993)

This case did not relate to rights to light, but it sets out the principles for the grant of interim mandatory injunctions which are also applicable to rights to light cases. The plaintiff claimed by way of interlocutory (interim) injunction, the delivery up of certain computer software following alleged repudiation of the contract by the defendant. If a mandatory injunction was refused, it was unlikely that the defendant would be in a position to pay damages to the plaintiff if the latter succeeded at trial. The judge considered whether the circumstances justified the ordering of a mandatory injunction. The following principles were set out which govern the grant of a mandatory interim injunction:

- The overriding consideration is which course of action (i.e. granting an injunction or not) is likely to involve the least risk of injustice if it turns out to be wrong.
- The court must keep in mind that an order which requires a party to take some positive step at an

interlocutory stage, may well carry a greater risk of injustice if it turns out to have been wrongly made than an order which merely prohibits action, thereby preserving the status quo.

- It is legitimate for the court to consider whether it feels a high degree of assurance that the plaintiff will be able to establish his right at a trial. That is because the greater the degree of assurance that the plaintiff will ultimately establish his right, the less will be the risk of injustice if the injunction is granted.
- Even where the court is unable to feel any high degree of assurance that the plaintiff will establish his right, there may still be circumstances in which it is appropriate to grant a mandatory injunction at an interlocutory stage. Those circumstances will exist where the risk of injustice if the injunction is refused sufficiently outweighs the risk of injustice if it is granted.

On the facts of the case, the judge considered that there was no doubt that, if no injunction was granted but the plaintiff was successful at trial, damages would be an inadequate remedy for the plaintiff, as the defendant had insufficient money to pay damages. He also considered that there was a risk that damages would not be an adequate remedy for the defendant, if an injunction was granted but the defendant was ultimately successful at trial, as it would be very difficult to quantify the defendant's losses. In deciding where the least risk of injustice lay, the judge took account of the fact that he felt a high degree of assurance that the plaintiff would succeed in establishing at trial that the defendant was in repudiatory breach of the contract. He therefore granted the plaintiff a mandatory interim injunction.

Mandatory interim injunctions requiring the defendant to pull construction work down have, on occasion, been granted. This has happened, for example, in cases where the defendant has deliberately speeded up his building works in an attempt to prevent an injunction being granted to stop him.

Daniel v Ferguson (1891)

The plaintiff owned a long lease on a property which adjoined land owned by the defendant. After inspecting plans showing proposed building works on the defendant's land, the plaintiff feared that a proposed wall would interfere with his rights to light. He therefore issued a writ and made an application for an interim injunction preventing the development from going ahead. The defendant received notice on the Saturday that an injunction was going to be applied for the following Friday. He immediately set a large number of men to work, worked all night and nearly all Sunday so that by Monday evening, the wall was already up to 39 ft. At the hearing of the injunction application, the judge ordered the defendant to stop building and to remove the wall he had built from his land. The defendant appealed.

The Court of Appeal considered whether the judge had been entitled to order an interim mandatory injunction which would result in the defendant taking down an otherwise perfectly sound wall until the matter was finally disposed of at trial. It held that the judge was justified in making his order. It found that to order otherwise would encourage people to speed up and complete their building works in the hope that, once they were up, the court would be reluctant to order them to be pulled down.

Von Joel v Hornsey (1895)

The plaintiff owned a house opposite the defendant's land, on which the latter was rebuilding his house. The plaintiff warned the defendant that, if the building continued, he would start proceedings to obtain an injunction to stop him infringing the plaintiff's rights to light. The work continued and the plaintiff issued proceedings. However, the defendant evaded service of the court proceedings and in the meantime continued building the house until finally the proceedings were served on him. The judge ordered an interim mandatory injunction, requiring the defendant to pull down that part of the building which had been built after the plaintiff had warned him he intended to bring an action. The defendant appealed.

The Court of Appeal dismissed the appeal. It considered that the defendant had deliberately tried to avoid service in order to hurry on the building, in defiance of the plaintiff's objection and of the court. Lindley LJ stated that builders who were willing to take the chance of speedily putting up a building in such circumstances, must also run the risk of pulling it down.

7.4.1.3 Enforcement of undertakings in damages

As set out above (at 7.4.1), a claimant who obtains an interim injunction will almost always need to give an undertaking in damages. If he subsequently fails to establish his right to a final injunction at trial, the court has a discretion whether to enforce the undertaking, i.e. to require the claimant to pay to the defendant the loss he has suffered as a result of the interim injunction being made. Undertakings will generally be enforced except in special circumstances.

Cheltenham and Gloucester Building Society v Ricketts (1993)

In this case, which concerned allegations of mortgage fraud by the plaintiff building society against the defendants, the Court of Appeal set out a number of principles relevant to undertakings in damages. These included the following:

- Except in exceptional cases, an undertaking in damages is the price which the person asking for an interim injunction has to pay for its grant. The court cannot compel an applicant to give an undertaking but it can refuse to grant an injunction unless he does.
- The undertaking does not create a cause of action. It does, however, enable the party who is subject to the interim injunction to apply to the court for compensation if it is subsequently established that the interim injunction should not have been granted.
- In a case where it is later decided that the injunction should not have been granted, the undertaking is likely to be enforced, although the court retains a discretion not to do so.
- The time at which the court should determine whether or not the interim injunction should have been granted will vary from case to case. Where (as happens in many cases) the injunction remains in force until the trial, the question

of the propriety of its original grant and the enforcement of the undertaking will not be considered before the conclusion of the trial.

- The damages recoverable by enforcement of the undertaking will generally be awarded on a similar basis to damages awarded for breach of contract.

Lunn Poly Ltd v Liverpool & Lancashire Properties Ltd (2006)

The defendants were freehold owners of a shopping centre. Unit 28 was leased to the claimants. The defendants bricked up a fire door. The judge granted the claimants an interim injunction entitling them to reinstate the fire door and preventing the defendants from interfering with it. The claimants gave an undertaking in damages. At the trial, the same judge held that bricking up the fire door had been a breach of the lease, but he did not grant a final injunction. Instead, he ordered damages. The defendants applied to enforce the claimants' undertaking as to damages. The judge refused to enforce the undertaking on the basis that the defendants' conduct in bricking up the door had been provocative and unlawful; that they had changed their position by the time of the trial; that they had brought the interim injunction on themselves and that they had only avoided the grant of a final injunction at trial by agreeing to conditions which they had previously refused.

The Court of Appeal stated that as a matter of general principle and general practice, where a claimant has obtained an interim injunction and the court decides at trial that a permanent injunction should not be granted, the defendant can normally expect, virtually as of right, to be able to enforce the undertaking. However, it accepted that there are exceptions to the general rule where there are special circumstances. The Court of Appeal held that, in this case, the judge had been entitled to reach the decision not to enforce the undertaking.

Regan v Paul Properties Ltd (2006)

The claimant was the owner of a maisonette in Brighton. He claimed that the defendant's development infringed his rights to light and applied for an interim injunction. Instead of an injunction, the defendant agreed to provide undertakings not to increase the height of the buildings before the conclusion of the trial. In return, the claimant gave an undertaking in damages. At trial the judge decided that the claimant was not entitled to a final injunction, but awarded damages instead. The defendant therefore applied to enforce the claimant's undertaking in damages so as to recover the losses caused by the interim injunction. The losses had been estimated at £160,000. The judge's decision on the final injunction was reversed by the Court of Appeal (see 7.4.2 below), but his decision on the undertaking in damages remains interesting.

The judge decided, in the exercise of his discretion, not to enforce the claimant's undertaking in damages for a number of reasons: the defendant's actions had been unlawful; the defendant had continued to assert that there would be no actionable interference with rights to light even though the claimant's surveyor had demonstrated to it that this was not correct; the defendant had acted without prudence in continuing the development in the face of the claimant's protests and it ran the risk of the precise damage which had in fact happened; the claimant acted in good faith in applying for an interim injunction and it had not been wrongly obtained, simply because at trial the judge decided that damages should be awarded instead; the law on whether a mandatory injunction should be granted was unclear; the claimant was going to suffer financial hardship as a result of a previous costs order made and it would be unjust for him to suffer any further as a result of the profits from the development being lower than they would otherwise have been, due to the claimant's reliance on a right to light.

7.4.2 Final injunctions

Final injunctions are granted at the trial of the action.

At the trial, in many cases the question will be whether the court should award a final injunction or damages instead (often referred to as 'damages in lieu'). A final injunction, unlike an interim injunction, is permanent and the court's decision is made after hearing submissions and witnesses, who will be cross-examined where appropriate. The court decides whether to award an injunction or damages by exercising its discretion in accordance with the principles laid down in case law. As the judge will have heard all the evidence, the risks of injustice which exist in relation to interim injunctions no longer exist. The test for whether to award a final injunction or damages is therefore different from the test for an interim injunction. The leading case on the circumstances in which a court will award damages instead of a final injunction is *Shelfer v City of London Electric Light Co* (1895).

A final injunction may be either prohibitory or mandatory (as to which, see 7.4.1 above).

Shelfer v City of London Electric Light Co (1895)

This was not a rights to light case, but it set out the principles relevant to whether an injunction or damages should be ordered in cases of nuisance, including rights to light. An electric lighting company (the defendant) erected powerful engines near to property, which was owned by the plaintiffs in one action (the freehold owners and reversioners) and leased to the plaintiff in a second action. Owing to excavations for the foundations of the engines and to vibration and noise from the engines when installed, structural damage was caused to the house and annoyance and discomfort caused to the lessee. The defendant intended substantially to increase the engine power in the future. The plaintiffs started actions for final prohibitory injunctions to stop the defendant's engines and to prevent it from continuing to damage the plaintiffs' property and for damages. The judge decided that the company had created a nuisance, but refused to grant an injunction, awarding damages instead. He held that, despite the fact that there was inconvenience, in particular on the top floors of the property, and that the plaintiff lessee might have to make arrangements to sleep elsewhere, damages were fair compensation. The plaintiffs appealed against the refusal of an injunction.

The Court of Appeal allowed the appeal and granted an injunction. A.L. Smith LJ pointed out that where a person commits a nuisance, he is not entitled to ask the court to sanction it, by purchasing his neighbours' rights by the payment of damages. The starting point (or the prima facie position), where the plaintiff's legal rights had been invaded, was that an injunction should be granted. Although this was the starting point, the plaintiff might disentitle himself from claiming an injunction by conduct or delay (sometimes called laches). On the other hand, the defendant might disentitle himself by his conduct, from paying damages instead of an injunction being awarded. This might occur, for example, if he acted with reckless disregard of the plaintiff's rights or speeded up the building works to complete before an injunction could be granted. With that background, A.L. Smith LJ set out what he described as a good working rule for the circumstances in which damages would be awarded rather than an injunction, namely:

- if the injury to the plaintiff's legal rights is small;
- if the injury is capable of being estimated in money;
- if the injury can be adequately compensated by a small money payment; and
- if it would be oppressive to the defendant to grant an injunction.

On the facts of the case, the Court of Appeal decided that the injury to the plaintiff tenant was not small and nor was it capable of being estimated in money. He had a 19-year lease with the prospect of continuing annoyance, inconvenience and discomfort from the noise and vibration of the engines. In the case of the freehold owner, an injunction was also granted as the effect of the engines was, and would continue to be, to cause damage to the property.

The guidelines in the *Shelfer* decision (often called the *Shelfer* 'working rule') have been applied in many cases, including rights to light cases, for more than a century. The Court of Appeal in a rights to light case (*Regan v Paul Properties Ltd* (2007)) has recently confirmed that the *Shelfer* decision is still binding. The *Shelfer* working rule has also recently been described in a rights of way case (*Jacklin v Chief Constable of West Yorkshire* (2007) (see 7.4.2.1 below)) as a 'hallowed and reliable working rule'.

Cowper v Laidler (1903)

The plaintiffs had acquired rights to light over the defendant's adjoining premises. The defendant intended to construct buildings which would materially diminish the light received by two of the plaintiffs' windows. The plaintiffs brought proceedings against the defendant claiming a prohibitory injunction preventing the defendant from constructing his building so as to infringe the plaintiffs' rights to light. The defendant argued that the value of the buildings which he proposed to put on his land would be much higher than the value of the plaintiffs' cottage. He also argued that the plaintiffs had only bought the last few shares in their cottage because they knew that it would become very valuable and therefore they would be able to get a high price for it. On this basis, the defendant argued that an injunction would be oppressive in that it would effectively compel him either to buy the cottage at an unreasonable price or to abandon his proposed building works.

The judge granted the injunction restraining the defendant from building so as to obstruct the two affected windows. He held that the defendant's proposed building would materially interfere with the plaintiffs' rights to light to these windows. He pointed out, relying on *Shelfer*, that a plaintiff was entitled to an injunction unless there were special circumstances (such as delay) or unless the injury was trivial or the damages would only be small. He also pointed out that to refuse an injunction and to award damages instead effectively compels the plaintiff to part with his right to light for money. The judge decided that it was not oppressive to award an injunction. It was no more oppressive for the defendant to have to buy the plaintiffs' property at the full price, taking account of the right to light, than for the defendant to say that he must be allowed to build in disregard of the plaintiffs' right.

Colls v Home and Colonial Stores Ltd (1904)

This case is the main case on infringement of rights to light (see Chapter 5). The plaintiffs (Home and Colonial Stores) were the lessees of a building opposite the defendant's land. The plaintiffs brought an action for an injunction claiming that the defendant's proposed building would obstruct their right to light. The judge held that the proposed building would not so materially interfere with the light previously enjoyed by the plaintiffs as to amount to a nuisance and dismissed the claim. The plaintiffs appealed, but in the meantime the defendant had built his development. The Court of Appeal granted an injunction ordering the defendant to remove the building he had now constructed. The defendant appealed to the House of Lords.

The House of Lords reversed the Court of Appeal's decision to award a final mandatory injunction. Lord Lindley stated that the general rule, that where a legal right is infringed an injunction ought to be granted, was subject to the qualifications referred to in *Shelfer*. He considered that, even assuming that the plaintiffs had a claim for nuisance, damages would be very small and would be an adequate remedy. On the other hand, granting a mandatory injunction in such a case would be unduly oppressive. Lord Macnaghten stated that an injunction was necessary where the injury could not fairly be compensated in money, if the defendant's conduct had been high-handed, an attempt to steal a march on the plaintiff or to evade the jurisdiction of the court. On the other hand, he considered that, where it was not clear whether there was a nuisance at all and the defendant had acted fairly, an injunction should not be granted. He also pointed out that the court ought not to allow plaintiffs to use protection of their rights to light as a means of extorting money from their neighbours or as a means of oppression.

Slack v Leeds Industrial Co-operative Society Ltd (1924)

The plaintiff owned commercial premises on one side of a square and the defendants owned commercial premises on the opposite side. The plaintiff had a right to light over the defendants' premises. The defendants pulled down their buildings and started to rebuild them to a greater height and size. Before the buildings were complete, the plaintiff's solicitors wrote to the defendants asking them to disclose details of the plans. From the plans it was clear that the completed buildings would interfere with the plaintiff's rights. The plaintiff claimed an injunction restraining the defendants from building in this way. The judge found that the defendants' building would interfere with the plaintiff's rights to light but that the injury would be small and capable of being calculated in money. Applying the rule in *Shelfer*, he found that this was a case where damages should be awarded instead of an injunction. However, he believed that he did not have jurisdiction to award damages instead of an injunction because the buildings had not yet been built and, therefore, no wrong had yet been committed. He therefore awarded an injunction. This issue was referred to the Court of Appeal and then the House of Lords. The House of Lords decided that the judge was entitled to award damages. The case then returned to the Court of Appeal to decide whether an injunction or damages should have been awarded.

The Court of Appeal decided that damages should have been awarded. The judge's findings, which the Court of Appeal held were justified by the evidence, brought the case within the working rule in *Shelfer*. The injury would be small, was capable of being calculated in money and the award of an injunction would be oppressive to the defendants.

Tamares (Vincent Square) Ltd v Fairpoint Properties (Vincent Square) Ltd (2007)

The claimant's and defendant's properties were adjacent. The defendant carried out a redevelopment. The claimant claimed that the new building would interfere with the light to four of its ground floor windows: two were the entrance lobby windows and two were by the basement stairs. It claimed a mandatory injunction, requiring demolition of a significant part of the defendant's new building. The judge applied the test in *Shelfer*. He held that the injury to the basement stair windows was small, was capable of being estimated in money and could be adequately compensated by a small monetary payment. He also considered that it would be oppressive to the defendant to grant a mandatory injunction requiring demolition of part of its development. In making a decision on oppression, he took into account that the claimant had not applied for an interim injunction (as to which, see 7.4.2.1 below); that the injury was trivial and that a mandatory injunction requiring demolition would be wholly out of proportion to the injury caused; that the defendant had acted honestly and had believed throughout, not unreasonably (on expert advice), that its development would not infringe any right to light.

Regan v Paul Properties Ltd (2007)

The claimant was the owner of a maisonette in Brighton. The defendant proposed to construct a mixed commercial and residential development opposite the claimant's property. The claimant started an action claiming that the development would interfere with his rights to light. He claimed a mandatory injunction, requiring the defendant to cut back one of the units in the proposed development. The judge decided that the claimant was not entitled to an injunction and awarded damages instead. The claimant appealed.

The Court of Appeal applied the working rule in *Shelfer*. It expressed the view that this case was binding on the Court of Appeal and that it was authority for five propositions:

- A claimant is prima facie entitled to an injunction against a person committing a wrongful act, such as a continuing nuisance, which invades the claimant's legal right.
- The wrongdoer is not entitled to ask the court to sanction his wrongdoing by purchasing the claimant's rights by payment of damages, assessed by the court.
- The court has jurisdiction to award damages instead of an injunction, but this does not mean that the court is to legalise wrongful acts by a defendant.
- The court's discretion to award damages instead of an injunction should be exercised in accordance with well-settled principles and not so as to deprive a claimant of his prima facie right, except under very exceptional circumstances.
- Factors relevant to the exercise of the court's discretion include:
    - whether the injury to the claimant's right is small;
    - whether the injury can be estimated in money;
    - whether it can be adequately compensated by a small money payment;
    - whether it would be oppressive to the defendant to grant an injunction;
    - whether the claimant has shown that he only wants money;
    - whether the conduct of the claimant has made it unjust to give him more than a money judgment; and
    - whether there are any other circumstances which justify the refusal of an injunction.

Applying *Shelfer*, the Court of Appeal decided that there was not a small injury to the claimant's right to light for his living room: the area receiving adequate light would be 42–45% instead of 67%. Although the injury could be compensated in money, it could not be adequately compensated by a small money payment. The loss in value was £5,000–£5,500 and this was considered not to be a small figure. In addition, the sum of compensation which the claimant could expect to get if negotiating the release of his right to light, when linked to the profits of the development, would not be small. The Court of Appeal held that an injunction would not be oppressive to the defendant, although it would involve reducing the proposed size of one of the units in the development. The court took into account the conduct of the defendant in taking a calculated risk, with its eyes open, to continue with the development (even though this had been on expert advice), after the claimant had objected.

As set out above, the courts in many cases have followed the working rule in the *Shelfer* case. However, inevitably as the law has developed over the last century, in some cases the courts have departed from the working rule and, on occasion, been less willing to grant an injunction than they would have been if the working rule had been applied. This has happened as recently as 2005 (in *Midtown*). In the light of the Court of Appeal decision in *Regan* (see above), it is thought that such an approach is wrong. It seems likely that the Court of Appeal in *Regan*, if it had decided the *Midtown* case, would have ordered an injunction.

Midtown Ltd v City of London Real Property Company Ltd (2005)

The freehold and leasehold owners of a property brought actions against the defendant in relation to its proposed development of the adjacent site. The claimants asserted that the defendant's proposals would interfere to a substantial degree with their rights to light. They claimed a final prohibitory injunction preventing the defendant from building so as to interfere with their right to light; alternatively, damages. The judge held that the defendant had infringed the claimants' rights to light, except in relation to one part of the land. He found that the reductions to the available light as a result of the development would be 'very large': it would reduce the percentage of the rooms which were adequately lit to single figure percentages from percentages greater, on average, than 50%.

The judge refused both the freeholder and the leaseholder injunctions, allowing a claim for damages instead. In doing so, he expressed the view that an earlier Court of Appeal decision showed a willingness on the part of the courts to depart from the four requirements in the *Shelfer* case in an appropriate case. His reasoning in relation to the freeholder was that:

- it was only interested in the property from a money-making point of view. If the value of the property had been diminished, this could therefore be compensated by money;
- it had probably not suffered any loss at present, as it had the benefit of the existing lease;
- it had its own plans for redevelopment, which would be likely to make the injunction academic;
- the defendant had behaved reasonably and openly, whereas the claimants had not acted reasonably, including not answering letters; and
- it would be oppressive to the defendant to be prevented from pursuing a worthwhile and beneficial development.

In relation to the leaseholder, which occupied the property, the judge also took into account that its employees always used artificial light when using the offices.

7.4.2.1 Conduct of the claimant

The House of Lords in *Shelfer* (see 7.4.2 above) made it clear that the conduct of the parties could affect whether a final injunction or damages would be awarded. Relevant conduct of the claimant includes delay, failure to apply for an interim injunction or acquiescence. A claimant may not apply for an interim injunction because he simply leaves it too late to do so or because he does not want to take the risk of giving an undertaking in damages. A claimant may acquiesce in the defendant's development for a period of time before starting proceedings. These factors may prevent a claimant from being awarded a final injunction. This is particularly likely to be the case where the delay has resulted in the building being constructed before the trial (at which a decision will be made about whether to award a final injunction). The issue of the claimant's conduct has arisen in rights to light cases, but also in cases relating to breaches of covenant and rights of way.

Wrotham Park Estate Co Ltd v Parkside Homes Ltd (1974)

The defendant built a number of new houses on its land, which was on the Wrotham Park Estate, in breach of a covenant with the plaintiff. The plaintiff then began an action, claiming an injunction to restrain building works and a mandatory injunction requiring demolition of any buildings already constructed in breach of covenant. The plaintiff did not apply for an interim injunction, partly because it did not wish to give an undertaking in damages. By the time of the trial, the new houses had been sold and the new owners (who were joined as defendants) were living in them. The plaintiff argued that, despite its failure to claim an interim injunction (which could have prevented the houses being built), it should be entitled to a final mandatory injunction (to pull them down). It argued that the plaintiff had chanced its arm in continuing to build after a letter of complaint and the commencement of the court action and that the new owners had bought in full knowledge of the risks and taken out insurance policies to cover them for the risks.

The judge considered that it was an important factor that the defendant continued with building operations in the face of clear, early protest and the commencement of a court action. He accepted that the plaintiff's decision not to apply for an interim injunction did not necessarily prevent it obtaining a final mandatory injunction. However, in this case, he considered that it would be 'an unpardonable waste' to pull down the much needed houses. Later in the judgment, he described the reasons for his refusal of an injunction to demolish the houses as social and economic. He also took into account that the plaintiff had not suffered any financial loss and that the construction of these houses did not prevent the enforcement of the covenant in relation to other parts of the Estate. Instead of an injunction, the judge made an award of damages.

Blue Town Investments Ltd v Higgs and Hill plc (1990)

The plaintiff owned a property with a right to light over the defendant's adjoining land. The defendant was building a block of flats on its land and the plaintiff alleged that the construction would interfere with its rights to light. The parties negotiated and the plaintiff appeared to accept the defendant's proposal to pay compensation for the infringement. Surveyors were instructed and valued the compensation at approximately £7,500. On the basis that the plaintiff was happy for the defendant to continue with the work if it paid compensation, the defendant continued to build. However, six months later the plaintiff claimed an injunction ordering the defendant to pull down the flats or refrain from building them in a way which interfered with its rights to light. The plaintiff did not apply for an interim injunction as it wanted to avoid giving an undertaking in damages, which due to the scale of the project could have been very substantial. This put the defendant in a very difficult position since it had spent huge sums of money on the development and would not know whether it was permitted to build until the trial of the action. The defendant applied to strike out the plaintiff's claim for a final injunction as being vexatious.

The judge held that, although the plaintiff's case was not unarguable, its chances of obtaining an injunction at trial were minimal. The judge decided that, by a letter to the defendant some seven months before proceedings had started, the plaintiff had elected to seek compensation instead of requiring the development to be altered. Thereafter, he found that the plaintiff had stood by, without protest, while the defendant proceeded with the work. He considered that it would be very difficult for the plaintiff to establish at trial that it had not acquiesced in the development. Standing by and watching a party proceeding on the basis that rights would not be enforced was, in his view, the sort of conduct which disentitled a plaintiff from claiming an injunction. He therefore decided that the claim should be struck out unless the plaintiff was prepared to apply for an interim injunction and to give an undertaking in damages.

Deakins v Hookings (1994)

The plaintiff had acquired a right to light over the defendant's adjoining property. The defendant wished significantly to extend her property. At an early stage, the plaintiff wrote a letter complaining that the new building would interfere with her light. However, although she consulted a solicitor, proceedings were not started until the defendant's building work had been completed. At this stage, it was too late to apply for an interim injunction to prevent the building work being carried out. The plaintiff claimed that there was interference with the light to her kitchen and living room and sought a final mandatory injunction, requiring demolition of part of the defendant's new extension. It took seven years for the action to get to trial.

In considering whether to grant a mandatory injunction (to remove part of the first floor of the defendant's property, which would involve redesigning and constructing the defendant's bathroom), the judge took into account the delay and the plaintiff's failure to apply for an interim injunction. He held that, although the plaintiff had not started proceedings promptly, she had asserted her rights in correspondence and had not acquiesced in the interference with her light. He then considered the working rule in *Shelfer* and decided that the loss of light was not small and that damages were not an adequate remedy for the sort of loss of amenity suffered. The plaintiff's loss was less devastating than the defendant's (redesign and reconstruction of the bathroom), but was sufficiently significant to justify an injunction.

Gafford v Graham (1999)

The defendant converted a bungalow on his land to a two storey house, extended a barn and built a riding school in breach of covenants with the plaintiff. In answer to the plaintiff's action for breach of covenant, the defendant argued that the plaintiff had acquiesced in the work and that, as a result, he was entitled to no remedy at all (whether an injunction or damages); alternatively, that the acquiescence meant that he was entitled only to damages.

The Court of Appeal held that the plaintiff had acquiesced in the work to the bungalow and the barn, by making no complaint until three years afterwards. His claim for an injunction and damages therefore failed altogether. In relation to the riding school, the plaintiff had complained promptly. However, he had made no application for an interim injunction. The Court of Appeal found that this was an important factor to be taken into account in deciding whether a mandatory injunction to demolish the building should be granted at trial. It held that, as a general rule, someone who, with the knowledge that he has enforceable rights and the ability to enforce them, stands by whilst a permanent and substantial structure is unlawfully erected, ought not to be granted an injunction to have it pulled down. The Court of Appeal thought, in this case, that the failure to apply for an interim injunction might not have been enough, but a further factor tipped the balance in favour of the award of damages. That factor was that the claimant had agreed in correspondence that he was prepared to accept a cash settlement. Together with the fact that an injunction would be oppressive to the defendant, this was sufficient to mean that the plaintiff was only entitled to damages and not a mandatory injunction.

Mortimer v Bailey (2005)

The claimants owned and occupied a property adjacent to the defendants' house. In breach of a restrictive covenant with the claimants, the defendants began building a large extension to which the claimants had previously objected on the grounds of loss of light, loss of direct winter sunlight and loss of view. Work on the extension began in early June 2003. The claimants then wrote asking for the work to stop immediately and threatening legal proceedings. However, they did not start proceedings until the end of July, at which stage they applied for an interim injunction preventing the defendants from continuing with the work. The judge refused the application for an interim injunction, on the basis that only one more week's worth of construction works remained and, applying the test in *American Cyanamid* (see 7.4.1.1 above), that damages were an adequate remedy.

At the trial, the claimants claimed a mandatory injunction requiring the defendants to demolish the extension. The joint surveying expert's evidence was that the extension had affected the enjoyment of the kitchen/family room because of the loss of light, sunlight and view and that the overall effect was somewhat overpowering and claustrophobic. The judge held that the claimants had been reasonable in refusing to consent to the extension and that damages would not represent adequate compensation. He awarded a mandatory injunction, requiring the defendants to demolish the extension or to alter it so as to prevent it from affecting the free flow of light to the claimants' house and to prevent any loss in value of that house. The defendants appealed. Relying on *Gafford v Graham*, they argued that due to the claimants' delay in seeking an interim injunction, they should not be entitled to a final injunction.

The Court of Appeal dismissed the defendants' appeal. Peter Gibson LJ did not think it appropriate to say that a person who did not apply for an interim injunction, but has made clear his intention to object to the breach and to bring proceedings for the breach, should be debarred from obtaining a final injunction. He considered that, in appropriate circumstances, it may be entirely reasonable for a claimant, having told the defendant of his objection, to proceed to trial rather than taking the risk (including giving an undertaking in damages) of interim injunction proceedings. The failure to seek an interim injunction promptly was a factor to take into account in deciding whether to grant a final injunction. However, this case was not one in which the claimants' conduct disentitled them to an injunction. It was different from *Gafford v Graham* because the claimants had not suggested that they would be willing to receive damages instead of an injunction. They had not stood by while the extension was built. The defendants had taken a gamble that it was unreasonable for the claimants to object to the extension: they had lost the gamble.

Jacklin v Chief Constable of West Yorkshire (2007)

The defendant carried out substantial construction work on its land and, in the course of this work, obstructed a path over which the claimant had a vehicular right of way. The claimant sought an injunction requiring the defendant to remove the obstruction and to restore the traffic flow. The evidence was that the claimant was aware of the defendant's intentions in 1997, that the defendant carried out the works in 1997 and 1998, but that the claimant did not protest in writing until 2000 and did not start proceedings until 2002. The judge granted him a final mandatory injunction. This would have required the defendant to change the traffic flow on its land, to allow the current exit to operate as an entrance and to move a storage container blocking the right of way. The defendant appealed, arguing that damages should have been awarded instead of an injunction. The defendant argued that, as the claimant had delayed in bringing proceedings, he should not be granted a mandatory injunction. The defendant also argued that the working rule in *Shelfer* meant that an injunction would not be granted if three of the four parts of the working rule were decided in the defendant's favour.

The Court of Appeal held that the claimant was entitled to a mandatory injunction and that the judge had exercised his discretion properly. On the question of delay, as the judge had held, the defendant knew that the claimant claimed a vehicular right of way from an early stage, but had proceeded regardless. The Court of Appeal also held that the four parts of the working rule in *Shelfer* were cumulative and therefore the defendant had to satisfy each of the four hurdles to prevent the award of an injunction. The defendant had not done so, as the judge had found that the award of an injunction would not be oppressive to the defendant.

7.4.2.2 Conduct of the defendant

Conduct of the defendant may disentitle him from successfully arguing that damages should be awarded instead of a final injunction. A.L. Smith LJ in *Shelfer* (see 7.4.2 above) gave examples of where the defendant has acted in reckless disregard of the claimant's rights or has speeded up the building works so that they are completed before an injunction can be granted. The same point was made by Lord Macnaghten in *Colls* (see 7.4.2 above), where he said that an injunction might be necessary if the defendant has acted in a high-handed manner, if he has endeavoured to steal a march on the claimant or to evade the jurisdiction of the court.

Pugh v Howells (1984)

The plaintiffs and defendants owned adjoining properties. In 1981, the defendants obtained planning permission to build an extension to their property. The plaintiffs objected to the planning application and thereafter wrote stating that the extension would infringe their rights to light and that, if the defendants went ahead, they would have no alternative but to apply for an injunction. The following year, the defendants were advised by a chartered surveyor that the proposed extension would interfere with the plaintiffs' right to light to their kitchen. In April 1983, the plaintiffs noticed that the defendants were pulling down a lean-to and their solicitors therefore wrote to the defendants asking them to disclose any plans. The defendants made an unhelpful reply. A further letter sent to the defendants by recorded delivery was returned by the defendants marked 'not accepted'. Before the plaintiffs could take further action, there was a bank holiday weekend. During this weekend, the defendants' builders returned and built the extension up to roof level. Immediately thereafter, the plaintiffs started court proceedings, claiming a mandatory injunction requiring the defendants to take down the extension so that it did not interfere with their rights to lights. The judge held that although there was an actionable nuisance, damages would be a more appropriate remedy. The plaintiffs appealed.

The Court of Appeal reversed the judge's decision, granting the plaintiffs a mandatory injunction. It referred to the House of Lords' decision in *Shelfer*, saying that a court needed not just to look at the working rule, but also what the House of Lords had said about the conduct of the parties. It was clear in this case that, where the defendants had been warned more than once that what they were doing would be resisted by an application to court, where in spite of the warnings and in spite of advice from their own surveyor, they carried on and took the risk of building, they could not complain if the result was that they were ordered to pull down part of the building. The Court of Appeal considered that the plaintiffs' conduct was perfectly reasonable: as soon as they saw the lean-to coming down, they asked for information. However, the defendants acted unreasonably and high-handedly: their response to the first letter was unhelpful, they refused to accept delivery of the second letter and they went ahead with the work over a bank holiday weekend, leaving the strong impression that they were hurrying on with the work to try to achieve a fait accompli before the plaintiffs could challenge them in court. In addition, the defendants had not satisfied the working rule in *Shelfer*. The injury was not small, it was difficult to say that it could adequately be compensated in damages and, having regard to the conduct of the defendants, it would not be oppressive to grant an injunction. A mandatory injunction was therefore awarded requiring the defendants to remove the part of the extension above ground floor level.

7.5 DAMAGES

There are two types of damages which a court can award at trial:

- damages in substitution for an injunction; or
- common law damages.

An account of profits (which is a remedy requiring the defendant to hand over all his profits) is unlikely to be available for interference with rights to light.

7.5.1 Damages in substitution for an injunction

Under section 50 of the *Supreme Court Act* 1981 the court has power to award damages in addition to or in substitution for an injunction. The section provides:

> 'Where the Court of Appeal or the High Court has jurisdiction to entertain an application for an injunction or specific performance, it may award damages in addition to, or in substitution for, an injunction or specific performance.'

As a result of section 38 of the *County Courts Act* 1984, County Courts have the same power. The power was originally established by section 2 of the *Chancery Amendment Act* 1858, now repealed, which is often referred to as 'Lord Cairns' Act'. Damages awarded in substitution for an injunction are often described as 'damages in lieu' and, on occasion, as '*Wrotham Park* damages'.

7.5.1.1 General principles: *Wrotham Park*

The general principles for the assessment of damages awarded in substitution for an injunction have been set out in cases relating to interference with easements or restrictive covenants. The starting point is the decision in *Wrotham Park Estates Co Ltd v Parkside Homes Ltd* (1974). The principles are equally applicable to rights to light cases. Essentially, the court considers what would have been the result of a hypothetical negotiation (before the interference occurred or breach was committed) between a willing seller and willing buyer, prepared to agree a proper price but not a ransom sum, for the release of the restrictive covenant or rights to light. The outcome of the hypothetical negotiation is often a percentage of the profit of the development or of the benefit of the development to the defendant. The particular percentage applicable in each case will depend on the facts and, in the cases referred to below, has varied from 5% to 50%. In cases where there is no or insufficient evidence of the likely profit of the development, the court will do its best to assess a fair figure and to arrive at a deal that 'feels right'.

Wrotham Park Estate Co Ltd v Parkside Homes Ltd (1974)

The developer defendant built a number of houses in breach of covenant. For the reasons explained in 7.4.2.1 above, the judge did not award an injunction. Instead, he said that that the plaintiff should be compensated in damages.

The defendants argued that damages should be nil or nominal, as the Wrotham Park Estate had not been diminished in value by the building works. The judge considered that awarding nominal damages in place of a mandatory injunction which would have restored the plaintiff's rights would not do justice to the case. He held that a just substitute for a mandatory injunction would be such a sum of money as might reasonably have been demanded by the plaintiff from the builder as a quid pro quo for relaxing the covenant. The plaintiff argued that this sum should be a half to a third of the development value. The judge held that in such a case the landowner, faced with a request from a developer which he feels reluctantly obliged to grant, would first have asked the developer what profit he expected to make from his operations and then reasonably have required a percentage of the anticipated profit as the price for the relaxation of the covenant. In this case, the judge took into account that the covenant did not have a commercial or even nuisance value, that the breach of covenant affected only a very small area of the Estate and that its impact on the Estate was insignificant. He thought that, on the facts of the case, the court should act with great moderation and held that 5% of the developer's anticipated profit would be fair. He ordered that payment of this sum should be apportioned between the 14 new owners and the developer.

Bracewell v Appleby (1975)

The defendant owned one of six houses which had a right of way over a private road. He built another house on an adjoining plot. The plaintiffs, who were owners of other houses in the road, began proceedings for a declaration that the defendant had no right of way for the new house and for an injunction restraining the defendant from using the road to reach it.

The judge held that although the defendant did not have a right of way over the private road to the adjoining land, the plaintiffs were not entitled to an injunction as a result of their delay in taking action and assessed damages instead. The judge held that the defendant was liable to pay an amount of damages which, so far as it could be estimated, was equivalent to a proper and fair price which would be payable for the acquisition of the right of way. The plaintiffs were to be treated as being willing to accept a fair price for the right of way and not as if they were in the extremely powerful bargaining position which an interim injunction would have given them. The judge assessed the notional profit that the defendant had made on the new house as £5,000. He went on to say that the proper approach to damages was to arrive at a fair figure which the parties would have arrived at to compensate the plaintiffs for loss of amenity and increased use of the road and, at the same time, which would not be so high as to deter the defendant from building at all. He took into consideration that it was a time of increasing property prices, that the defendant was not a speculative builder and that he had built the new house to live in (and did live in it, having sold the old house). The judge held the defendant would have paid a relatively large proportion of the notional profit to get the right of way and achieve the building of his new home and assessed the figure at £2,000 (i.e. 40% of the notional profit). The plaintiffs were entitled to one-fifth each of this sum as damages.

Jaggard v Sawyer (1995)

In breach of covenant, the defendants built a property on a residential development in a private cul-de-sac. The plaintiff, who owned another house in the development, began proceedings when the building was at an advanced stage and did not seek an interim injunction. The judge refused to award her a final injunction and awarded damages instead. He made an award of damages based on the sum the defendants might reasonably have paid for a right of way to the new house and the release of the covenant. He awarded the plaintiff, as one of the nine owners of houses in the cul-de-sac, a ninth share of this amount. The plaintiff appealed.

The Court of Appeal upheld the judge's decision to award damages instead of an injunction. On the question of damages, it also upheld the judge's decision. The Court of Appeal agreed with the judge that the value of the right should be what a reasonable seller would sell it for. It held that in situations like this a plaintiff should not be treated as eager to sell but, on the other hand, that the court would not value the right at the ransom price which a very reluctant plaintiff might put on it.

Gafford v Graham (1999)

The defendant converted a bungalow on his land to a two storey house, extended a barn and built a riding school in breach of covenants of which the plaintiff had the benefit.

The Court of Appeal reversed the judge's decision to award an injunction in relation to the riding school and decided the issue of damages. It held that the *Wrotham Park* decision was the correct basis for assessing damages in such a case. In that case, there had been no diminution in value: however, the Court of Appeal considered that, in a case where there had been diminution in value, that could be taken into account in assessing the sum which could reasonably have been demanded as a quid pro quo for relaxing the restrictions. The plaintiff argued that damages should be assessed as the average of two methods of assessing the value of relaxation of the covenant: first, based on the income to be generated by the business and, secondly, on the marriage value between the land and the facility afforded by the riding school. The defendant argued for a lower sum based on 5% of the approximate cost of building the riding school. The Court of Appeal held that the question of damages in such a case was a matter of judgment and that the plaintiff's figures represented a far more realistic guide to the amount the plaintiff might reasonably have demanded for relaxation of the restrictions at the time the riding school had been built. It therefore awarded the sum proposed by the plaintiff as damages.

AMEC Developments Ltd v Jurys Hotel Management (UK) Ltd (2001)

The defendant constructed a hotel closer to the boundary with the claimant's land than the building line permitted by a restrictive covenant. The claimant began an action for breach of covenant. It was agreed that, as a result of the breach of covenant, the hotel had 25 additional rooms (265 rooms, rather than 240), although the defendant argued that other designs allowing more than 240 rooms would have been possible. The parties agreed that the appropriate method of assessing damages was to carry out a hypothetical negotiation in accordance with the judgment in *Wrotham Park*. However, they relied on extremely complex calculations of the benefit to the defendant of the additional 25 rooms, which varied vastly in amount. The judge identified a number of features the hypothetical negotiation would have, including:

- the claimant is a willing seller, but only at a proper price;
- the defendant is a willing buyer and prepared to pay a proper price, but not a large ransom;
- the parties in the negotiation would put forward their best points and take into account the other side's best points;
- the negotiations would be deemed to take place before any transgression occurs;
- the basis of the negotiation would be a split of the perceived gain to the defendant. That gain would not be obvious and would be the subject of debate, with variables;

- the parties would be taken to know the hotel's actual figures for the purpose of assessing gain;
- the negotiation would take place on the basis that the extent to which the defendant could build more than 240 rooms was not clear;
- the additional land was not just a few inches, but almost 4 m wide;
- the defendant would be fairly keen, though not overwhelmingly anxious, to have the right to build over the line; and
- the deal has to feel right. Negotiation science and rationality get one only so far.

The claimant's position was that damages should be 50% of a gain to the defendant of £3m (i.e. £1.5m). The defendant argued that the benefit to it was minimal or slight and they argued for 50% of £281,000, as the value of the extra 25 rooms (i.e. damages of approximately £140,000). Having considered at length the detailed expert evidence provided by the parties, the large differences between which he found difficult to reconcile, the judge assessed the result of hypothetical negotiations as £375,000. In doing so, he pointed out that the questions arising in relation to damages in such cases were matters of judgment which are incapable of strict rational and logical exposition from beginning to end.

Lane v O'Brien Homes Ltd (2004)

The claimant started an action for breach of an oral agreement that only three houses would be constructed on land sold by the claimant to the defendant. On the claimant's application for an interim injunction preventing the defendant from building a fourth house, the defendant undertook not to do so pending the trial. At trial, the judge awarded the claimant £150,000 damages (which was approximately half of his assessment of the defendant's building profit on the fourth house). The defendant appealed against the award, arguing that the damages were too high, that only a small proportion of the profit of the additional house should be ordered and that the judge had failed to take into account the construction cost of the fourth house in assessing the anticipated profit.

The appeal judge rejected the argument that there was a general principle that damages must be limited to a small percentage of the purchaser's potential profit arising from his breach of covenant. He took into account that the potential overall benefit to the defendant was not limited to the builder's profit, although he accepted that the builder's profit was much smaller than the judge had identified. He considered that the assessment should be at a later date than the contract for sale of the land, namely the date of planning permission. The assessment could not be at the time of building, as the fourth house was not built at the time of the trial due to the undertaking. He pointed out that the assessment of this form of damages was not a precise mathematical process, decided that the judge's assessment of the course of hypothetical negotiations was not wholly wrong and therefore dismissed the appeal.

7.5.1.2 Rights to light cases

The principles identified in the cases summarised above have also been applied in rights to light cases. In these cases, damages are calculated by reference to the amount a reasonable seller would receive in return for the loss of the right to light. The hypothetical negotiation is again carried out taking into account the benefit of the development to the defendant. Judges often use percentages of the likely level of profits, although the appropriate percentage will depend on the particular facts of the case. In some cases (such as *Carr-Saunders*), where there is no/little evidence of the defendant's likely profit, the judge may award damages based on a suitable multiple of damages for diminution in value or loss of amenity and has to 'do his best' with the little evidence he has.

Deakins v Hookings (1994)

The plaintiff had acquired a right to light over the defendant's adjoining property. The defendant wished significantly to extend her property. The plaintiff claimed that there was interference with her light to the kitchen and the living room and sought a final mandatory injunction, requiring demolition of part of the defendant's new property.

The judge decided that there was an actionable interference in relation to the lounge and awarded a mandatory injunction (see 7.4.2.1 above).

The judge also considered the question of damages in case there was an appeal. There was no appeal, so the result of the case was that there was a mandatory injunction. However, his calculation of damages remains interesting. The experts for the parties had considered damages on the basis of simple diminution in value of the property as a result of the loss of light. The plaintiff's expert had assessed this as £1,500. The judge held that damages in a case where they were to replace an injunction which would otherwise have been granted, should be awarded on the basis of the principles in the *Wrotham Park* case. He considered that if a plaintiff was to lose his right to light, he should be compensated for losing it on some basis that represented a fair price for being bought out. He held in this case that 5% (the percentage awarded in *Wrotham Park* would be too low) and that the right figure was 15% of the defendant's benefit from the development.

Carr-Saunders v Dick McNeil Associates Ltd (1986)

The plaintiff's building was opposite the defendant's premises in Covent Garden. The defendant increased the height of his building and the plaintiff started an action claiming damages for the obstruction of light to two windows on the second floor. The judge decided that the defendant's building works had caused a substantial interference with the plaintiff's light to the second floor.

On the question of damages, the parties' experts had given evidence as to the diminution in value (capitalising the rental value of the premises). On this basis, the figure which the judge preferred was approximately £3,000. The judge, however, considered that the correct approach to damages in rights to light cases, where damages were awarded instead of an injunction, was to follow the principles set out in *Wrotham Park*. He decided, therefore, that he was entitled to take into account the plaintiff's bargaining position and the amount of profit which the defendant would expect to make from the development. However, he had no evidence of loss of profit. He therefore considered he was entitled to take into account general loss of amenity: not only the loss of direct light, but also sky visibility, a pleasant view, etc. The absolute minimum figure was £3,000 and doing the best he could, on the basis of little evidence, he awarded damages of £8,000.

Marine & General Mutual Life Assurance Society v St James' Real Estate Co Ltd (1991)

The plaintiff and defendant companies owned adjoining properties. The defendant proposed reconstructing its property and the plaintiff claimed damages for interference with its right to light. The judge applied the principles in *Wrotham Park* and *Carr-Saunders*. He held that he was entitled to take account not only of the actual loss of light, but also the loss of amenity generally, owing to factors such as sky visibility, the impression that the building at the rear was now closer, the loss of sunlight and the general deteriorating quality of the environment. He was also entitled to take into account the plaintiff's bargaining position because, unless the plaintiff was bought off, the defendant's development would be inhibited. He assessed damages on the *Wrotham Park* basis, by relying on a comparable transaction where a payment of £25,000 had been made in return for the adjoining owner withdrawing his objections to the development. The position of the adjoining owner in the comparable transaction was somewhat stronger and the judge awarded £18,000 to the plaintiff in this case.

Tamares (Vincent Square) Ltd v Fairpoint Properties (Vincent Square) Ltd No 2 (2007)

The claimant's and defendant's properties were adjacent. The defendant carried out a redevelopment. The claimant claimed that the new building would interfere with the light to four of its ground floor windows: two were the entrance lobby windows and two were by the basement stairs. It claimed a mandatory injunction, requiring demolition of a significant part of the defendant's new building. The judge did not grant a final injunction and assessed damages in relation to the basement staircase windows instead.

The parties agreed that the correct measure of damages was the greater of (i) damages for loss of amenity to the dominant owner and (ii) damages to compensate for the loss of the ability to obtain an injunction. The evidence of rights to light experts was that the loss of amenity was very low: a maximum of approximately £3,000. The claimant also produced expert evidence on estimated profit of the development, which gave an average of £174,500. The judge held that he had to find the result of a hypothetical negotiation between the parties, normally at the date of breach. He set out the principles he considered applicable:

- the overall principle is that the court must attempt to find what would be a fair result of a hypothetical negotiation between the parties;
- the context, including the nature and seriousness of the breach, must be kept in mind;
- the right to prevent a development (or part of a development) gives the owner of the right a significant bargaining position;
- the owner of the right with such a bargaining position will normally be expected to receive some part of the likely profit from the development (or relevant part);
- if there is no evidence of the likely size of the profit, the court can do its best by awarding a suitable multiple of the damages for loss of amenity. (This appears to be a reference to the calculation in *Carr-Saunders*.);
- if there is evidence of the likely size of the profit, the court should normally award a sum which takes into account a fair percentage of the profit;
- the size of the award should not in any event be so large that the development (or relevant part) would not have taken place had such a sum been payable; and
- after arriving at a figure which takes into consideration all the above and any other relevant factors, the court needs to consider whether the 'deal feels right'.

He dismissed the defendant's arguments that only the loss of amenity should be awarded as the damage was trivial and that an uplift should be made from the loss of amenity (as in *Carr-Saunders*), rather than using a percentage of the profit. As to profits, he considered that 5% of the development profits (the percentage awarded in *Wrotham Park*) would be too low and that 40% (the percentage awarded in *Bracewell v Appleby* (1975)) would be too high. His conclusion was that hypothetical reasonable commercial people would take the half-way point between the two figures for the profit, namely £174,500, and then agree to a prima facie split of one-third (i.e. £58,166). Taking into account the context of the relatively modest nature of the infringement and the need to have a sum which would not put the defendant off the relevant part of the development, they would reduce it to £50,000 as a fair result. He then considered whether the deal felt right and concluded that it did. He therefore awarded damages of £50,000.

7.5.1.3 When damages in substitution will not be awarded

Courts can only award damages in substitution for an injunction where they have jurisdiction, at the date of commencement of the proceedings, to award an injunction. The question is whether, at the date the action is begun, the court *could* have granted an injunction, not whether it *would* have done (see *Jaggard v Sawyer* (1995) and *Harris v Williams-Wynne* (2006)). The court will not have jurisdiction to award an injunction (or damages in substitution) where the claimant has acquiesced in the defendant's conduct so that it would be unconscionable for him to continue to enforce rights which he had at the date of the breach.

Gafford v Graham (1999)

The defendant converted a bungalow on his land to a two storey house, extended a barn and built a riding school in breach of covenants of which the plaintiff had the benefit. In answer to the plaintiff's action for breach of covenant, the defendant argued that the plaintiff had acquiesced in the work and that, as a result, he was entitled to no remedy at all (whether an injunction or damages).

The Court of Appeal held that the plaintiff had acquiesced in the work to the bungalow and the barn, by making no complaint until three years afterwards. His conduct had been such as to make it unconscionable for the plaintiff to continue to enforce the rights he had had three years earlier. His claim for an injunction and damages therefore failed altogether.

Harris v Williams-Wynne (2006)

The claimant had built on land in breach of a covenant of which the defendant had the benefit. The claimant's claim was for breach of contract and the defendant counterclaimed for damages for breach of covenant. The defendant's counterclaim was for damages in substitution for an injunction, although he did not actually make a claim for an injunction. The claimant argued that the defendant had acquiesced in the construction of the building and that, therefore, he was not entitled either to an injunction or to damages in substitution for an injunction. The judge considered that the defendant's delay had deprived him of the possibility of an injunction. However, he held that there had not been acquiescence which prevented him from claiming damages in substitution for an injunction. The claimant appealed. The Court of Appeal dismissed the claimant's appeal. In this case, it was not unconscionable for the defendant to seek to rely on his legal rights.

It also appears that, where a court would have refused to award an injunction on the grounds of the claimant's unreasonable conduct, an award of damages on the basis of *Wrotham Park* may be inappropriate.

Forsyth-Grant v Allen (2008)

The claimant owned a hotel adjacent to the defendant's land and claimed that the construction of two houses on that land interfered with her rights to light. The claimant did not claim an injunction, but claimed an account of the defendant's profits (see 7.5.3 below). However, the judge and the Court of Appeal also considered *Wrotham Park* damages.

The judge held that, in view of the claimant's unreasonable conduct (which included a failure to reply to the defendant's offer of compensation or to allow the defendant's surveyor the opportunity to inspect the hotel), the court would not have awarded an injunction and that, therefore, an award of damages calculated on the basis of *Wrotham Park* or *Carr-Saunders* was inappropriate. The Court of Appeal stated that, as this finding was not challenged on appeal, there was no need to express a view about whether it was correct. Having made this finding, the trial judge assessed damages on the basis of the loss actually suffered by the claimant, which amounted to the capitalised diminution of the letting value of the rooms whose light was affected by the defendant's development. This amounted to £1,848.63.

7.5.2 Common law damages

If a claimant is not entitled to damages in substitution for an injunction (see 7.5.1.3 above), he may still be entitled to damages at common law. Damages at common law for nuisance, including interference with rights to light, are measured by reference to the diminution in value of the premises. It is often the case that the diminution in value of the premises is far less than the value of the right to light in the hypothetical negotiation which will be undertaken where damages are assessed in substitution for an injunction. The diminution in value will usually be assessed by capitalising the rental value of the property or part of the property affected by the loss of light.

Forsyth-Grant v Allen (2008)

The claimant owned a hotel adjacent to the defendant's land and claimed that the construction of two houses on that land interfered with her rights to light. The judge rejected the claimant's claim for an account of profits (see 7.5.3 below) and, also, refused to assess damages on the basis of *Wrotham Park* (see 7.5.1 above). He therefore assessed damages on the basis of the loss actually suffered by the claimant, which amounted to the capitalised diminution of the letting value of the rooms whose light was affected by the defendant's development. This amounted to £1,848.63. Unusually, in this case, the damages assessed on the basis of diminution in value were greater than they would have been on the basis of a *Wrotham Park* negotiation. The judge assessed 15% of the profit as the appropriate percentage which he would have allowed on the *Wrotham Park* basis: this gave a figure of only £1,050.05. These findings were not challenged in the Court of Appeal.

7.5.3 Account of profits

An account of profits is a remedy which requires the defendant to hand over all the profits he has made to the claimant. It is used primarily in cases where the defendant is under a fiduciary duty to, and in a relationship of trust with, the claimant. It is also used in some intellectual property cases. It is different from damages assessed on a *Wrotham Park* basis, where the claimant receives the percentage of the defendant's profits which is the outcome of a hypothetical negotiation (see 7.5.1 above). The Court of Appeal has confirmed that an account of profits is unlikely to apply in cases of nuisance, including rights to light. If such a remedy was ever available, it could only be awarded in exceptional circumstances.

Forsyth-Grant v Allen (2008)

The claimant owned a hotel adjacent to the defendant's land and claimed that the construction of two houses on that land interfered with her rights to light. The claimant did not claim an injunction, but claimed an account of the defendant's profits.

In the Court of Appeal, Patten J stated that there was no decided case in which an account of profits had been available as a remedy in a nuisance claim. Therefore, the judge would have been entitled to reject the claim for an account of profits on the basis that it was not an available remedy in an action for nuisance. Even if it could ever be an available remedy, it would be necessary to show exceptional circumstances and there had been no such circumstances in this case.

8
High hedges

8.1 INTRODUCTION

The remedies for interference with rights to light discussed earlier in this book are available only in limited situations. In particular:

- rights to light do not apply to all properties – but only to those where such rights have been acquired by one of the methods set out in Chapters 2 and 3;
- rights to light relate to buildings, not to gardens (see 1.1 above); and
- there is no right at common law to a view (see 1.1 above).

High hedges, particularly when made up of leylandii (Leyland Cyprus or *X cupressocyparis leylandii*), have been perceived as a serious problem for a number of years. These shrubs can grow by 4 ft in a year and reach a height of 100 ft or more. They can soon diminish light in neighbours' gardens or throw houses and gardens into the shade. Neighbour disputes over such hedges are extremely common.

Stanton v Jones (1994)

This neighbour dispute ran for some 24 years. It began in about 1971 when Mr Stanton planted a row of ten leylandii on his land about 1 ft from the boundary between his house and that of Mr Jones. When the hedge reached 15 ft, Mr Jones complained his garden was being robbed of sunlight. In 1979, when the row of conifers was 25 ft, formal complaints via solicitors began. The hedge eventually reached a height of 35 ft. Mr Jones' house was only 35 ft from the boundary. Mr Stanton eventually agreed to trim the hedge back to about 25 ft. However, Mr Jones then cut it down by 5 ft (and there was a dispute as to whether he had cut it down considerably further) without his neighbour's agreement. Mr Stanton began proceedings in the Birmingham County Court claiming damages for trespass because Mr Jones had gone on to his land, without his consent, and cut back the trees. Mr Jones claimed that he was entitled to do so for the purpose of maintaining and trimming the trees in accordance with the 'scheme of management' in place on the estate. The scheme provided that hedges on and along the boundary were deemed to be party walls and were to be kept properly trimmed and in good condition. The judge in the County Court made a declaration that, in accordance with the scheme, the hedge was deemed to be a party wall, that Mr Jones was entitled to maintain it and that he had the right to reduce its height. Mr Stanton appealed. The Court of Appeal agreed with the judge that the hedge was a party wall. However, it referred the case back to the County Court to decide whether Mr Jones had the right to cut it back as far as he had. The County Court then awarded Mr Jones a declaration entitling him to cut the hedge and in 1996 the conifers were reduced to 12 ft.

The decision in *Stanton v Jones* is not applicable generally to other neighbour disputes relating to leylandii. Mr Jones was successful because there was a 'scheme of management' in place on the estate and, in accordance with this scheme, hedges on and along the boundary were deemed to be party walls and were to be kept properly trimmed and in good condition. In the absence of such a scheme, it is difficult to see that, at common law, he would have been entitled to cut back the hedge (see 7.2 above).

At common law, it is theoretically possible that a claimant could:

- make a claim for interference with his rights to light caused by a high hedge. This would only succeed if he had a right to light and if he could demonstrate actionable interference with the light to his building. Such a claim would not apply to the garden (see above);
- make a claim in the tort of nuisance, not relying on a right to light, on the basis that the height of the hedge prevented him from enjoying his property to the full. However, such a claim would be far from straightforward.

8.2 HIGH HEDGES LEGISLATION

From the late 1990s, the government took steps to investigate the problem of high hedges. It was concerned about a possible 17,000 problem hedges in England and Wales which could lead to disputes like that in *Stanton v Jones*. The concerns included the loss of light to neighbouring houses and gardens and the blocking of views caused by leylandii hedges. The government reviewed whether it would be possible to apply or extend the existing law to cover these problems. The possibilities included extending rights to light, amending planning law so as to require planning permission for hedges and amending the *Environment Protection Act* 1990 (which deals with 'statutory nuisances') to include high hedge problems. After consultation, it was decided that the best method of dealing with the problem would be to introduce a new statutory method of control over high hedges.

After a number of private members' bills relating to high hedges had not been passed by Parliament, the government introduced a procedure for dealing with complaints concerning high hedges on neighbouring land as Part 8 of the *Anti-social Behaviour Act* 2003 (sections 65–84). Part 8 came into force in England on 1 June 2005 and in Wales on 31 December 2004.

The *Anti-social Behaviour Act* 2003 (ASBA 2003) allows complaints to be made to the local authority by an owner or occupier of domestic property who claims that his reasonable enjoyment of the property (or that of a prospective occupier) is adversely affected by the height of a high hedge situated on land owned or occupied by someone else. There is provision for appeals in ASBA 2003 and in the *High Hedges (Appeals) (England) Regulations* 2005 and the *High Hedges (Appeals) (Wales) Regulations* 2004. In addition, guidance to individuals and local authorities on the operation of the system has been issued by the Office of the Deputy Prime Minister (now the Department for Communities and Local Government (DCLG)). The guidance includes Building Research Establishment (BRE) guidelines for calculating whether hedges are likely to cause significant loss of light to neighbouring houses and gardens.

There are a number of key issues:

- the meaning of a high hedge;
- who may complain;
- the procedure for making a complaint;
- whether the reasonable enjoyment of the property is adversely affected;
- remedies;
- appeals;
- powers of entry; and
- criminal offences and enforcement.

8.3 A HIGH HEDGE

Section 66 of ASBA 2003 sets out what is meant by a high hedge. It is so much of a barrier to light or access as:

- is formed wholly or predominantly by a line of two or more evergreens; and
- rises to a height of more than 2 m above ground level.

However, a line of evergreens is not to be regarded as forming a barrier to light or access if the existence of gaps significantly affects its overall effect as such a barrier at heights of more than 2 m above ground.

An evergreen means an evergreen tree or shrub or a semi-evergreen tree or shrub. As explained in the DCLG guidance *High Hedge Complaints: Prevention and Cure,* ASBA 2003 does not only apply to leylandii. Evergreen trees and shrubs also include conifers and laurel. The term semi-evergreen is not defined in ASBA 2003, but means that the hedge retains some live foliage throughout the year and could include privet.

8.4 WHO MAY COMPLAIN?

A complaint may be made by an owner or occupier of a domestic property. Domestic property is defined in section 67 as:

- a dwelling

A dwelling is any building or part of a building occupied or intended to be occupied as a separate dwelling. The Act, therefore, relates to flats as much as to houses; or

- a garden or yard which is used and enjoyed wholly or mainly in connection with a dwelling.

This contrasts with the position in relation to rights to light claims, which apply only to buildings.

8.5 THE PROCEDURE FOR MAKING A COMPLAINT

A complaint must be made to the local authority for the area in which the high hedge is situated. First, however, the complainant must take all reasonable steps to resolve the problem without complaining to the local authority. The local authority may decide not to proceed with the complaint, if it considers that the complainant has not taken all such reasonable steps or if the complaint is frivolous or vexatious. If the local authority decides to proceed, it must then decide:

- whether the height of the hedge adversely affects the complainant's reasonable enjoyment of his property; and if so
- what action, if any, should be taken with a view to remedying the adverse effect or preventing its recurrence.

Local authorities are entitled to charge a fee for dealing with complaints. A number of local authorities do not charge. Some others currently charge as much as £650.

8.6 WHETHER THE REASONABLE ENJOYMENT OF THE PROPERTY IS ADVERSELY AFFECTED

The Act does not provide any guidance on how an owner demonstrates that his property is being adversely affected by the height of a high hedge. However, *High Hedge Complaints: Prevention and Cure* identifies a non-exhaustive list of factors a local authority may consider, including:

- privacy. The guidance states that, in general, the level of privacy provided by a 2 m high hedge is what might reasonably be expected;

- shelter;
- noise, smell and smoke;
- damage to plants;
- overhanging branches;
- litter dropped by the hedge;
- obstruction of light to windows. The BRE guidelines on *Hedge height and light loss* identify a method for calculating the appropriate height of an evergreen hedge in order to allow to the windows of a house the amount of daylight and sunlight recommended in the British Standard, BS 8206 Part 2, *Lighting for buildings: Code of practice for daylighting*;
- obstruction of light to gardens. The BRE guidelines also provide a method of calculating whether an evergreen hedge is likely to cause a significant loss of light to a neighbouring garden. BS 8206 Part 2 does not apply to gardens;
- visual amenity. This includes issues such as views, how close the hedge is to buildings and how dominant it is;
- the effect of gaps in the hedge; and
- public amenity.

The guidance also advises the local authority to obtain submissions from both parties and to hold a site visit. It should weigh up the harm caused by the hedge against its amenity value to the hedge owner and the community. The assessment should be made objectively, i.e. by assessing the impact of the hedge on the enjoyment by a reasonable person of his home and garden.

8.7 REMEDIES

If the local authority decides that action should be taken, it must, as soon as reasonably practicable, issue a remedial notice implementing its decision in accordance with section 69 of ASBA 2003. A remedial notice must state the initial action to be taken in relation to the hedge and any preventative action that the local authority considers must be taken thereafter. The action specified in the remedial notice must not require or involve either reducing the height of the hedge to less than 2 m above ground level or the removal of the hedge. A notice could therefore include an initial reduction in the height of the hedge and longer-term preventative action such as regular pruning or thinning out of dense branches. A remedial notice must set a reasonable period within which compliance is to take place.

A local authority may withdraw a remedial notice or waive or relax a requirement in it. The Act does not identify the circumstances in which it may do so. Some guidance is given by *High Hedge Complaints: Prevention and Cure*. It may be appropriate to waive, relax or withdraw a remedial notice if, for example, it contains an error, the parties have agreed a different solution to the problem or if there has been a material change in circumstances (such as a development on the land).

A remedial notice is binding on every owner or occupier of the land on which the hedge is situated. It takes effect as a local land charge, which is a charge registered against the land.

8.8 APPEALS

Appeals are dealt with by sections 71–73 of ASBA 2003, the *High Hedges (Appeals) (England) Regulations* 2005 and the *High Hedges (Appeals) (Wales) Regulations* 2004.

Appeals may be made against any remedial notice issued by the local authority or the decision to issue, or not to issue, a remedial notice. They may also be made against any decision to waive or relax any requirements of a remedial notice. Appeals must be made within 28 days and are made to the Secretary of State in England and the National Assembly in Wales. The appeal functions of the Secretary of State are carried out by inspectors from the Planning Inspectorate. The appeal may be allowed or dismissed in whole or in part. The remedial notice may be quashed or its requirements varied. On the other hand, if the appeal is against a decision of the local authority not to issue a remedial notice, the appeal authority may issue a remedial notice on behalf of the authority.

There is no further appeal against the decision of an Inspector. A party wishing to challenge such a decision would need to bring court proceedings for judicial review. Judicial review proceedings are different from an appeal. The court reviews the lawfulness of the decision, including whether it was unreasonable, irrational or an abuse of power.

There is also no appeal against the local authority's decision not to consider the complaint on the grounds that the complainant has not taken all reasonable steps to resolve the problem without making a complaint or that the complaint is frivolous or vexatious (see 8.5 above). In such a case, it may be possible to refer the decision to the local authority's complaints officer or the Local Government Ombudsman or, if necessary, to apply to the court for judicial review.

8.9 POWERS OF ENTRY

Section 74 of ASBA 2003 also allows a person authorised by the local authority to enter land in order to obtain information required for the purpose of determining whether the provisions of ASBA 2003 apply, whether to issue or withdraw a remedial notice, whether to waive or relax its requirements and to determine whether a remedial notice has been complied with. Similar powers of entry are given to the appeal authority. Twenty-four hours' notice must be given to every occupier before the power to enter is exercised.

8.10 CRIMINAL OFFENCES AND ENFORCEMENT OF REMEDIAL NOTICES

It is a criminal offence, punishable by a fine not exceeding level 3 on the standard scale (£1,000), intentionally to obstruct a person exercising the power to enter.

It is also a criminal offence, again punishable by a fine not exceeding level 3 on the standard scale, for a person to fail to take action on a remedial notice within the period stated for compliance. On conviction, the court may also order the offender to take steps to secure compliance with the remedial notice. Failure to do this is a further offence, punishable by a fine.

Where action is not taken to comply with a remedial notice, ASBA 2003 also provides that a person authorised by a local authority may enter the land and take the required action. If this happens, the local authority may recover any expenses reasonably incurred from any person who is an owner or occupier of the land. These expenses are a local land charge and bind successive owners and occupiers of the land.

8.11 GUIDANCE

The DCLG has issued guidance for individuals, local authorities and appeal authorities on how to deal with problems with high hedges. The guidance documents include:

- *Over the Garden Hedge*;
- *High Hedges: Complaining to the Council*;
- *High Hedges Complaints: Prevention and Cure*;
- *High Hedges: Appealing Against the Council's Decision*; and
- BRE guidance note: *Hedge Height and Light Loss.*

Index

The *Case in Point* series

The *Case in Point* series is a popular set of concise practical guides to legal issues in land, property and construction. Written for the property professional, they get straight to the key issues in a refreshingly jargon-free style.

Areas covered:

Party Walls
Item code: 7269
Published: May 2004

Estate Agency
Item code: 7472
Published: July 2004

Rent Review
Item code: 8531
Published: May 2005

Expert Witness
Item code: 8842
Published: August 2005

Lease Renewal
Item code: 8711
Published: August 2005

VAT in Property and Construction
Item code: 8840
Published: September 2005

Construction Adjudication
Item code: 9040
Published: October 2005

Dilapidations
Item code: 9113
Published: January 2006

Planning Control
Item code: 9391
Published: April 2006

Building Defects
Item code: 9949
Published: July 2006

Contract Administration
Item code: 16419
Published: March 2007

Construction Claims
Item code: 16978
Published: December 2007

Easements and Other Rights
Item code: 17245
Published: March 2008

Negligence in Valuations and Surveys (2nd edition)
Item code: 17550
Published: August 2008

Service Charges (2nd edition)
Item code: 17456
Published: August 2008

Tendering and Procurement
Item code: 17631
Due to publish late 2008